# The Widow

# Directed

# to

# the

# Widow's God

by

John Angell James

"Let thy widows trust in me."
Jeremiah 49:11

**Soli Deo Gloria Publications**
*...for instruction in righteousness...*

**Soli Deo Gloria Publications**
P.O. Box 451, Morgan, PA 15064
(412) 221-1901/FAX 221-1902

*

*The Widow Directed to the Widow's God* was
published in 1841 in London by
Hamilton, Adams, and Company.
This Soli Deo Gloria reprint is 1996.

*

ISBN 1-57358-035-X

# PREFACE.

ONE of the errands on which the Son of GOD came from heaven to earth, was to bind up the broken-hearted, and to comfort all that mourn : and during his sojourn upon earth, the tenderest sympathy was one of the virtues which adorned that holy nature, in which dwelt, as in its temple, "all the fulness of the Godhead bodily."

Like their Divine Master, the ministers of the gospel ought to be sons of consolation, and to perform the functions of a comforter, as well as those of an instructor : for if pure and undefiled religion, as regards the professors of christianity, consists, in part, of visiting the widow and fatherless in their affliction, how much more incumbent is it on its teachers, to cherish and to manifest the same tenderness of spirit towards this deeply suffering portion of the human family. A group of children gathered round a widowed mother, and sobbing out their sorrows, as she repeats to them, amidst many tears, their father's loved and honoured name, is one of those pictures of woe, on which few can look with an unmoistened eye.

Is it not strange, then, that with claims upon our sympathy, so strong and so generally acknowledged,

A 2

such mourners should have engaged no pious author to produce a separate treatise for their relief? That while the department of hortatory theology is so rich in its stores of consolation for the afflicted in general, the *widow* should have had no tribute of sympathy specially prepared to meet *her* sad case? At least I know of none. Popular treatises of inestimable value, such as Cecil's "Friendly Visit to the House of Mourning;" Grosvenor's "Mourner Comforted;" and Hill's "Faith's estimate of Afflictive Dispensations," published by the Religious Tract Society, under the title "It is Well;" are known by thousands to their consolation, and are, of course, as appropriate to the widow as to any other of the varieties of mourners—but *she* needs a special message of comfort from her Lord; a voice which speaks to her case alone; a strain of consolation which, in its descriptions and condolence, is appropriate, and exclusively so, to her. As it is the peculiarity of our sorrows which often gives them their depth and pungency, so it it is the peculiarity of sympathy also which gives to this cordial for a fainting spirit, its balmy and reviving power. Affliction, like bodily disease, has numerous varieties; and, comfort, like medicine, derives its efficacy from its suitableness to the case.

In Dr. ADAM THOMPSON'S "Consolations for Christian Mourners," there are two excellent sermons addressed to widows; but these constitute no exception to the statement, that there is no separate work for such mourners. May the present attempt, specially addressed to them, by one who knows, he trusts, by experience, the value of the considerations he submits to others; by one who has been called in time past to weep, and is now trembling and weeping again, be blessed by the GOD of all consolation, for their comfort.

The following work is written with great simplicity, in sentiment and style: for it would be a mockery of woe to approach it with far fetched subjects; recondite discussion; cold logic; or artificial rhetoric. The bruised heart loves the gentlest handling, and the troubled spirit is soothed with the simplest music. The soul has no inclination, at such times, and in such circumstances, for any thing but the "sincere milk of the word," leaving the strong meat for other and healthier seasons.

The volume is rather more expensively printed than on some accounts is desirable, but as it is to come into the hands of some whose eyes are dim, either with age or weeping, I thought it best to select a large type, and present a clear, uncrowded page.

J. A. J.

*Edgbaston, March 9th.* 1841.

# CONTENTS.

# FIRST PART.

APPROPRIATE SUGGESTIONS TO WIDOWS.

# CHAPTER I.

## SYMPATHY.

A WIDOW! What a desolate name! If there be one amidst the crowd of mourners that tread the vale of tears, who above all others, claims our sympathy, and receives it, it is you who have laid down the endearing appellation of Wife, to take up that of Widow. It would be a mockery of your woe to say, "Woman, why weepest thou?" You *may* weep, you must, you ought. You are placed by Providence in the region of sorrow, and tears befit your condition. Let them flow, and mine shall flow with them, for if it be ever our duty to weep with those that weep, it is when the Widow is before us. The death-bed scene is still fresh in your recollection; the parting look, the last embrace are still present to your imagination. And oh! the sense of loss that

B

presses like a dead weight upon your spirit, and converts this whole busy world around you, into one vast wilderness. You have my tenderest condolence. The closest tie which bound you to earth has been severed. It seems to you as if there were nothing left for you to do upon earth but to weep. The husband's much loved image, if it hang not upon the wall, silent and motionless, is drawn upon the heart, for the imagination to gaze upon, and to remind you of your desolation. He whose absence but for a week or a day created an uneasiness which nothing could relieve but his return, is gone not for a day, or a week, or a year, but for ever. He is never to come back, to gladden the heart of his wife, and to bless his household.

It has been finely observed "that the loss of a friend, (and much more the loss of a husband,) upon whom the heart was fixed, to whom every wish and endearment tended, is a state of dreary desolation, on which the mind looks abroad impatient of itself, and finds nothing but emptiness and horror. The blameless life, the artless tenderness, the pious simplicity, the modest resignation, the patient sickness, and the quiet death, are remembered only to add value to the loss, to aggravate regret for what cannot be amended, to deepen sorrow for what cannot be recalled. Other evils, fortitude may repel, or hope may mitigate, but irreparable privation leaves nothing to exercise resolution, or flatter expectation. The dead cannot return, and nothing is left us here but languishment and grief."*

But it is not merely the loss of such a friend you have to mourn, but probably the means of your comfortable sustenance. Your husband was your provider, and the supporter of your babes. When he died all your prospects faded. The sun of your prosperity set upon his grave. Even when an ample fortune is left, it is a poor substitute for that friend whose decease covered the earth with sackcloth, and spread a pall over every terrestial scene; but what an aggravation of woe, what a dreariness is added to desolation, when the spectres of poverty and

* Dr. Thomson's Consolations for Mourners, p. 119.

want, or even the dark portents of care and privation, rise from a husband's grave. Perhaps even his labour, and skill, and patient perseverance, were but just sufficient to support the family; and what is the widow, unused, perhaps, to business, and untrained to hardship, to do alone? "It is," says Mr. BRUCE, "the climax of human sorrow, when the wife of youth is left to mourn the loss of an affectionate husband at the time when his well-formed schemes were advancing to maturity; so that, in addition to the care of providing for her rising offspring, some of whom never learned to lisp the name of father, she has to struggle with difficulties, which his sagacity and perseverance might have overcome."

Nor is it only the want of support, afflicted woman, you dread for yourself and your children, but the want of protection. You have seen enough of the world to know, how selfishness prevails over benevolence, and how little disinterestedness is to be expected from that multitude, in which are to be found so many who oppress the weak, and so many more that neglect the friendless. A thousand fears of insult and injuries rise in your perturbed mind, and you feel as if the tear of the widow, and the cry of the fatherless, will have little power to interest the busy, and to melt the iron heart of the unjust. Already, perhaps, you think you have received significant hints, not to be mistaken, even from the friends of your husband, that your expectations, even of counsel and advice, much more of other kinds of assistance, must be very limited. It is possible, however, that sorrow, solitude, and dependance, may have produced a sensitiveness on this subject, which makes you more suspicious and mistrustful, than you have need to be, and that after all, there is a larger portion of sympathy and generous intention, than you may be led to suppose.

To the widow of the departed christian, there is another ingredient in the cup of her sorrow, another aggravation of the loss she has sustained, and that is, she is deprived of her own spiritual comforter and companion; and if she be a mother, of the religious instructor and

guide of her children. He that was at once
the king, the prophet, and the priest of the
little domestic community, is removed. How
tenderly did he solve her doubts, relieve her
perplexities, and comfort her in her sorrows.
How sweet was it to take counsel with him on
the things of another world, and to walk to the
house of God in company. What sabbaths they
spent, and what sacramental seasons they enjoyed together. And then his nightly and
morning sacrifice at the domestic altar; his
fervent prayers, and his pious breathings for
his family: but that tongue is now silent
in the grave; those holy hands are now no
more lifted up to bless the household; that
mild sceptre of paternal rule has dropped.
Even *he*, good man, felt a dread and a trembling that sometimes almost overcame his faith
and trust, as he lay upon his death bed, and
anticipated the hour when he should leave his
children amidst the snares and temptations of
this dangerous world. I do not wonder that
you, his sad survivor, should feel your great
responsibility, as you look round on the be-

reaved circle, and remember that these young immortals are left to your sole guidance and guardianship. Often you say, as the tears roll down your cheeks, " It is not merely, nor chiefly, the care of their bodies, nor the culture of their minds, that makes me feel my sad privation, but the interests of their souls. I could eat my bread, if it were *only* bread, and drink my cup of cold water, and deal out bread and water to *them* with tolerable composure, if I could well discharge the duty I owe to their souls, and see them following their sainted parent to the skies : but oh ! the thought that my boys have lost a father to guide them along the slippery paths of youth, and form their character for time and eternity too ; and that at a season when his instructive example and advice were most needed ; this is the wormwood and gall of a widow's cup."

Afflicted woman, if sympathy be a balm for the wounds of your lacerated heart, you have it. Bad as human nature is, it is not so entirely bereft of the whatsoever things are lovely, as not to condole with *you*. It is not yours to

reproach, in the language of holy writ, the insensibility of a whole generation, and say, "Is
it nothing to you, all ye that pass by : come
see if there be any sorrow like unto my sorrow,
wherewith the Lord has afflicted me." This
little volume, at any rate, comes to you as a
comforter and a counsellor. One individual
has thought upon you ; and as a minister of
him, who wept at the grave of LAZARUS, and
who restored to the widow of Nain, her son,
when she was following him with a heart half
broken to the grave, he comes with more than
human sympathy, and earthly consolation. It
is balm from heaven he brings, and a divine medicine for your sick and sorrowful heart. It is
christianity, in the person of one of its ministers
that presents the cup of peace. O turn not
away from it, nor refuse to be comforted. Hush
then, the clamour of tumultuous thoughts; calm
the perturbations of your troubled spirit ; for
the voice of the Comforter can be heard only in
the silence of submission. Yes, even *your* grief
is susceptible of alleviation. I cannot break
open the tomb to undo the work of death, and

re-animate and restore the dust which lies sleeping there : I cannot replace by your side the
dear companion that has been torn from it : but
I can suggest topics, which, if you can sufficiently controul your feelings to ponder them,
are of such a nature, so soothing and sustaining,
that they will pluck the sting from your affliction, and enable you by GOD's grace, to bear up
with fortitude under a load, which would otherwise crush you to the earth. I am anxious at
once to possess you with the idea, that you ought
not to be, and need not be, inconsolable. Tenderly as I feel for you, and anxious as I am not
to handle roughly the wounds which have been
inflicted upon your peace, still I must remind
you, that you are not authorised to indulge
yourself in an unlimited liberty of grief; nor to
justify such an excess, by affirming that you do
well to be sorrowful even unto death. I beseech
you then to obtain leave of your agitated heart,
to listen to the gracious words of Him of whom
it is so beautifully said, " He comforteth those
that are cast down." In his name I speak to
you; and I speak of that which I have tasted,

and felt of the Word of GOD.  I too have been
afflicted like yourself, and have known, not by
observation merely, but by experience, what a
desolation and blank one single death can make
in the garden of earthly joys : and where in that
hour of dreariness and woe, the lonely spirit may
find a refuge and a home.

# CHAPTER II.

## SUBMISSION.

"BE still, and know that I am GOD." Such is the admonition which comes to you; and which comes from heaven. It is GOD himself that has bereaved you, through whatever second causes he has inflicted the blow. Not even a sparrow falleth to the ground without his knowledge, much less a rational and immortal creature. He has the keys of death, and never for a moment trusts them out of his hand: the door of the sepulchre is never unlocked but by himself. Though men die and drop as unheeded by many as the fall of the autumnal leaf in the pathless desert, they die not by chance. Every instance of mortality, that for example which has reduced you to your present sorrowful condition, is a separate decision of infinite wisdom. Whether therefore the death of your husband

was slow or sudden; at home or abroad; by
accident or disease; it was appointed, and all
its circumstances arranged by GOD. "Be still,
therefore, and know that he is GOD, who doeth
his will among the armies of heaven, and the
inhabitants of earth, nor allows any one to say
unto him, What doest thou?" Bow down before him with unqualified submission, and find
relief in acquiescence.

But what *is* submission to GOD? It is not
a stoical apathy; a state of mind that scorns to
feel; a proud refusal to pay the tribute of a tear
to nature's GOD, when he demands it. No:
chastened grief is allowed, is called for. Sorrow is one of the natural affections of the soul,
not to be uprooted, but cultivated. If we did
not feel our losses, we should not be the better
for them. Gentle and well directed grief, softens
our hard hearts, and prepares them for the impression of divine truth, just as showers in
spring mollify the ground, and meeten it for
the reception of the seed, and the process of
germination. But then you must repress inor-
dinate grief. Submission to the will of God,

while it allows reasonable sorrow, forbids that which is excessive. Give not yourselves *up* to sorrow. All passionate distress, such as shuts out consolation and refuses to be comforted, is high rebellion against the will of heaven. It is at once irreligious and unreasonable. It is more, it is destructive, for it is "the sorrow of the world that worketh death." Your health is now doubly precious, and your life doubly desirable, for the sake of your children. You alone have now to care for them, perhaps, to provide for them; and it is immensely important not to waste that strength and energy in consuming sorrow, which is necessary for their welfare. Excessive grief will not only unfit you for exertion, but it will incapacitate you from deriving any improvement from the stroke. The voice and lessons of GOD's providence will be unheeded, yea unheard, amidst the noise of your tumultuous sorrows. Restrain your feelings. Call in reason, and especially religion, to your assistance.

Submission forbids all passionate invective; all rebellious language; all bitter reflections on

second causes ; and all questionings about the
wisdom, goodness, or equity of Providence.
" I was dumb," said the Psalmist, " I opened
not my mouth ;" there is submission—" because
*thou* didst it ;" there is the ground of it.    It
is said of AARON, when both his sons were
struck dead before the Lord, he " held his
peace."    It was not the silence of stupor, or of
stubbornness, but of submission.    How striking
is the commendation passed upon JOB, when
it is said, in reference to his behaviour under
his complicated losses, " In all this JOB sinned
not, nor charged GOD foolishly."    He said
nothing irreverend, or rebellious against GOD.
But it is equally incumbent upon you, in order
to the performance of this duty, that you should
not only suppress all murmuring, and complaining *language*, but all thoughts and feelings of
this kind.    If while the tongue is silent, the
heart is full of rebellion, there is no acquiescence.    Many who would be afraid, or ashamed
to give *utterance* to their feelings of insubordi-
nation, still continue to indulge them.    The
abstinence from murmuring and repining *words*,

then, is not submission, unless the heart be still. We must not contend with God, nor fight against Providence within the breast, for "he searcheth the heart and trieth the reins of the children of men."

Submission is that state of the soul under afflictive dispensations of Providence, which produces an acquiescence in the will of God, as just, and wise, and good. It expresses itself in some such manner as the following; " I feel and deeply feel the heavy loss I have sustained, and nature mourns and weeps; but as I am persuaded it is the Lord's doing, who has a right to do as he pleases, and who is at the same time too wise to mistake, and too benevolent to put me to unnecessary pain, I endeavour to bow down to his will."

Such is submission; but how difficult! How hard the duty to acquiesce in an event, which has reduced you to such a state of desolation, that earth seems to have lost its principal charms. Difficult my afflicted friend it is, but not impossible. All things are possible with GOD, and what you cannot do in your own strength, you can in His. Multitudes *have* submitted, whose loss was as great, whose prospects were as gloomy as yours. I have heard the language ; I have seen the conduct of submission in widows' houses, and have admired the grace of GOD, as manifested in such persons, and in such circumstances. That grace is sufficient for *you*. Do not make up your mind, that submission is impossible for you ; on the contrary, be persuaded that it may, by God's help, become your privilege, as it unquestionably is your duty, to exercise it. Pray for it. Let this be the burden of your supplication to God, but let it be presented in faith ;

> O Lord my best desires fulfil,
>     And help me to resign,
> Life, health, and *husband*, to Thy will,
>     And make Thy pleasure mine.

In bringing you and others to this state of mind, God employs motives ; he places certain truths and sentiments before the mind of the afflicted and enables them to contemplate these principles with such fixed attention, as to admit their reasonableness and force, and under their soothing and powerful influence, to suppress the murmur, and hush every complaint to silence. Some of these I now present to your notice.

1. Consider God's indubitable and unlimited right to take from you the dear companion of your life.

Are we not all his creatures, over whom he has an absolute, and irresponsible controul? Has he acted the part of a ruthless invader of your domicile, and committed an aggression, which he can as little justify, as you could resist ? Is it an unauthorised spoliation? No. Painful as it is to you, it was not an unrighteous act in him. Shall he not do as he will with his own ? You received your husband, if you received him with right views, rather as a loan, than an absolute gift; as a favour lent to be recalled at any time, when the donor thought proper to do so. And now he has demanded it back again. Hearken to his expostuation; "Woman, I do you no wrong, in asking for what belongs to me. Have I deceived you ? Did I ever renounce my right, or

c

promise to forego my claim ; or even intimate
that I would not urge it, till you had arrived at
extreme old age ?    Be still, and know that I am
God."    Do not then contend with God.    Yield
to his sovereign will.    Submit to his disposal.

2. But this perhaps will be thought by some
like vinegar to a festering wound ; and it will be
felt as a harsh and feeble motive to submission,
to tell a mourning widow that God had a right
to take from her the desire of her eyes.    " Oh?"
she is ready to exclaim, " Is this all you can say
to me ?"    No : but it is the basis of every thing
else : and even this is said rather to awe the rebellious thoughts, to keep in check the turbulent
feelings, in order that silence and calmness being
obtained, softer and sweeter accents may be listened to.    Think then of his unerring wisdom.
He cannot mistake.    He does nothing at ran-
dom, nothing in haste, nothing in ignorance.
" He is wise in heart:" and his understanding
is infinite.    He worketh all things after the
*counsel* of his will.    He fills every thing with
the product of his all-wise mind ; yes, even your
bitter cup of sorrow.    " Verily he is a God that

hideth himself," but it is in the secret place of
his infallible wisdom. "His judgments are a
great deep," but it is a depth of unfathomable
knowledge. There is some wise end to be answered; some object worthy of himself to be
accomplished, in your bereavement. He may
not, and will not, perhaps, reveal it to you now,
for reasons which he can justify: but if it were
proper or possible for you to know it, you would
exclaim, "Oh the depth of the riches both of
his wisdom and knowledge! How unsearchable are his judgments, and his ways past finding out." If you could see the wisdom of his
plans, and it were then left to your choice to
take back your husband again from the grave,
you would not dare to do it, on account of the
disarrangement and disorder which you would
see must ensue. Have you not sometimes ab-
stracted something from your children, without
assigning any reason, or explaining to them
what it would be improper for them to know, or
impossible for them to comprehend, and required them to confide in your known prudence?
Is it too much for GOD to expect this confidence

from *you?* He *is* wise: confide in his wisdom.
The moment your thoughts are rising into rebellion, or sinking into despondency, repeat the
short, the simple, but the potent sentiment,
" God has done it, and God is wise."

3. Nor is this all: for God is good. His
name is Love. His wisdom is employed to fulfil
the purposes of benevolence. He is concerned
for the happiness of his creatures. " He does
not afflict willingly, nor grieve the children of
men." He takes no pleasure in the tears and
groans of his offspring, any more than earthly
parents do, but like them, he often sees it necessary to call for their tears. Did you never
exercise your kindness in taking from the hand
of a child, that which the babe would not surrender without weeping? Divine goodness,
when it is clearly understood in all its schemes
and motives, will be as clearly demonstrated in
what it takes, as in what it gives. Add these
two ideas together, infinite goodness, and infinite wisdom. Apply them both to God: believe that they really belong to him, and that
they were both concerned in your affliction, and

then murmur if you can.   Did we *really* believe
in the doctrine of Providence, and that he who
superintends its administration, unites to an
arm of omnipotence, a mind of infinite knowledge, and a heart of boundless love, submission
would be easy.   Is the sepulchre of a husband
the only place where his wisdom and love may
be doubted?   Are these glorious attributes
dead and buried in the grave of that beloved
man whom you have lost?   It is nothing that
you cannot understand how your present
melancholy circumstances can comport with
love : your children often found it as difficult
to harmonise *your* conduct with love ; but now
they are arrived at manhood, they clearly comprehend it, and admire the rich displays of ju-
dicious kindness with which your treatment of
them was replete.   The time of weeping and
suffering, and with it the time of ignorance, has
passed away, and now your paternal character
stands justified before them.   So shall it be
with you, when you have reached your maturity
in heaven, you will see the goodness of GOD
which was contained even in these painful dis-

pensations of providence, under which you now so bitterly suffer. Yes, GOD is good; do not doubt it. Every attribute of GOD's nature is a motive to submission; every view we can take of that nature, and our relations to him, is a reason why we should acquiesce in what he does. It is only when out of sight of him, that we can indulge in a rebellious murmuring, and a refractory resistance of his will; the moment we come back into his awful presence, and realise him as near, we feel subdued.

4. But the foundation of this state of mind is laid, not only in considering what GOD is, but *what* WE *are*. Murmuring and complaining have their origin in ignorance or forgetfulness of our sinful condition. None can truly submit to affliction which they do not feel they have deserved. The heroine, a widow, of what has been called one of the purest of our tragedies, is made to say, in the bitterness and pressure of her griefs, " Gracious heaven, what have I done, to merit such afflictions?" As long as you have such an opinion of yourself, there is, there can be, no submission. The very idea

that we do not deserve it, is rebellion against the will of heaven, and will inevitably lead to the most unholy and unchastised sorrow. It is only when we enter into the words of the Psalmist that we shall give up our murmurings and repinings, "He hath not dealt with us after our sins, nor rewarded us according to our iniquities." How meekly does the prophet submit to the chastening hand of God, under the subduing power of this one thought, "I will bear the indignation of the Lord, because I have sinned against him." "Wherefore should a man complain, a living man for the punishment of his sins." Oh sufferer, take this view of your case, and consider yourself a sinner. Call to recollection what sin is, an infinite evil, and deserving of an infinite punishment; an evil that might have long since consigned you to the abodes of interminable misery. Dwell upon the number, the aggravations, and the repetitions of your sins. Among other sins, perhaps, you may mention your ingratitude for, and misimprovement of, the mercy you have lost. You made your husband your God, inasmuch

as you loved him more than GOD : and can you
wonder that he is removed? "It is of the
Lord's mercies that you are not consumed, because his compassions fail not." Dare you
murmur, since you have only the rod, when you
might have had the curse? Does the language
of complaint become those lips, which might
have been pouring forth the petition for a drop
of water to cool your parched tongue? I deny
not the reality or the weight of your affliction :
I do not insult your griefs by affirming that
there is no cause for them. I admit you may
justly go mourning all your days ; but then I
contend it is a powerful motive to submit, to
consider that you might have been tormented
through all eternity : and that nothing has
a more powerful tendency to check the excess
of sorrow, than the consideration, that your
sins have justly merited all you have suffered,
ever will, or ever can suffer on earth.

5. But I may also mention that one of the
great ends of Providence in sending the affliction, is to *bring* you into a state of submission.
Perhaps you have never yielded your heart to

God. God spake to you in your prosperity, and you would not hear. You have tried to be independent of God. You have lived for yourself and not for God. You have never yet taken his yoke upon you. In the days of your fullness you yielded not your heart to him; and now he is calling you to yield to him in the time of your straits. As you would not submit to him amidst the joys of the married state, he has placed you in widowhood, and calls for submission there. "Surely she will resign herself to me now," is perhaps his declaration and expectation. How much is he set on producing this state of mind in you, when he takes such methods to accomplish it. Shall his end be defeated? Will you resist now? Will you carry on the conflict in your weeds? What, not yield now, broken, disappointed, forlorn, as you are? Will you be rebellious, not only in sight of the flowing fountain, but amidst the wreck and fragments of the broken cisterns; and contend against God, like JONAH, not only beneath the shade of the green and flourishing gourd, but before the naked stem of

the blighted and withered one ?   Oh woman,
submit to GOD, it is for this he has driven
thee into the wilderness, like HAGAR of old,
and 'mayest thou, like her, cease the conflict
there, and say " Thou God seest me.   Here
also have I looked after him who seeth me."

6. Among the motives to submission, should
be placed, *a due regard to your own comfort*.
It has been beautifully said, that the wild bird,
yet untamed and unaccustomed to confinement,
beats itself almost to death against the wires of
its cage, while the tame prisoner, quietly acqui-
esces, and relieves its solitude by a song.   An
apt illustration of the soothing influence of submission.   No possible relief, but a certain and
immense addition to the calamity is gained by
mourning and repining.   It is a vain and useless thing, as well as a sinful one.   It is of itself
a deep affliction, a sad discomposure of spirit, a
fever of the heart, a delirium of the soul, and is
so much added to the weight of the original
trouble.   But resignation to the dispensations
of GOD's Providence, what a blessed anodyne is
this to the soul ; what a sabbath from all those

sinful disturbances which discompose our spirits;
it is a lower heaven; a green and sunny spot in
a region of gloom, and desolation : for as in the
state of glory there is an unchangeable agree-
ment between the will of the Creator and of the
creature, so according to the same measure
wherein we conform our wills to GOD's now, we
proportionably enjoy the holiness and blessedness of that state. Daughter of sorrow, since
you can no longer enjoy the pleasure of possession, seek the comfort of submission. Extract
by resignation, the few drops of cordial, which
even your wormwood and gall contain. For-
bidden any longer to enjoy the sweetness of
gratitude for the retention of the boon, open
your heart to the tranquillising comfort of sur-
rendering it to GOD. Mollify the wounds of
your lacerated heart with the balm of acquiescence, and do not inflame them with the uncon-
trouled grief of a rebellious spirit. Try the effect
of those few sweet words, " Father! not my will,
but thine be done." They will be like the voice
of CHRIST, to the winds and waves of the stormy
lake : or like heavenly music to the troubled

mind.    There is no relief but in unqualified submission, and there is relief in that.

7. Perhaps you are a professor of religion,
and ought to find in that another and a powerful motive to this frame of mind.   You profess
to believe in GOD through CHRIST, and to consider him as the author of all your trials, as well
as of all your comforts ; to view him as your
Father ; to be assured that he loves you too well
to do you any harm ; to be confident that he is
making all things work together for your good.
Now then let us see the blessed influence of
your faith.   Let us behold in you the tranquillising power of your principles.   Should *you*
sorrow as do others ?   Should *you* appear as un-
controlable in your grief as those who know not
GOD.   A day or two since I visited a widow,
whose husband had been killed by the overthrow
of a carriage.   I found her as might be expected
deeply afflicted; but it was grief kept within due
bounds by the controuling power of eminent
piety, as dignified as it was deep, and there were
circumstances too, eminently calculated to produce a complicated sorrow.   Her calm, though

affecting distress attracted the attention of a lady whose brother had died awfully sudden. " Ah," she exclaimed, to my bereaved friend, "how differently did my sister-in-law act to what you have done. But *your* composure is the effect of religion. I see now the power of religion." Be it your study to exhibit the same power, and to draw forth the same testimony. Glorify GOD in the fires. Let it be your prayer that your religion may shine forth in all its lustre, and manifest itself in all its glory. Let it be one of your consolations to be enabled to do honour to the truth and grace of GOD in your support. Think what an effect a contrary spirit will have upon those who observe it. How many widows making a profession of religion, have by the violence of their grief astonished the observer of their conduct. It was not a scene or a season in which to utter the language of reproach, but who could help saying to them- selves, though delicacy kept them from saying to the sufferer, " Where in all this tumult of soul, and excessive grief, is their religion." Is there no help for them in GOD ? We expected

a calmer sorrow, from a christian. She does
not much commend religion to us."

18. Some of you may contrast your circumstances with those of others around you. Wrap
not your weeds upon you, and say, "Is there
any sorrow like unto my sorrow?" Is there?
Yes; and far greater. You have lost a good husband; but perhaps you have a comfortable support for yourself and your children,—there goes
the poor widow who has lost her support, as well
as her husband. You are left with fatherless
children, but they are kind and dutiful,—there is
a widow whose heart bruised by her loss, is well
nigh broken by the unkindness of an undutiful
son. Your children are all in health,—there is a
widow who pours her daily tears over a crippled
son, or a consumptive daughter. You are surrounded by a wide circle of sympathising friends,
—there is a widow, forlorn, alone, and a stranger
in this busy world. Oh it is well sometimes
to compare our sorrows with those of others.
What widow that shall read these pages can
speak of grief like the following?—

" A poor woman, from the north of England,

went with her family to seek employment in the parish of St. Mary-le-bone, London. The husband, through fatigue, was attacked with a bilious fever; the disorder soon assumed a very malignant, putrid character, of which he died. Two of the children caught the infection, and died also. The widow was reduced, with her surviving children, to the most deplorable poverty, and seemed on the point of starving. In this situation she was visited by a christian, who observed an old Bible, with a large print, lying on her table. He said, ' I perceive you can read, and have got the best of books by you.' She replied, ' Oh, sir, what should I have done without it ? It is not my own. My eyes are, with illness, anxiety, and tears, too weak for a small print : I borrowed this Bible of a neighbour. It has been food to my body as well as to my soul. I have often passed many hours without any nourishment, but I have read this blessed book, till I have forgotten my hunger.' Sometime after this the poor woman died, literally worn down and exhausted with want and anxiety ; but the night before she expired,

the consolations of the holy Scriptures shone in
her countenance.    She spoke of her dissolution
with a smile of sacred triumph; enumerated
her pious ancestors and acquaintance, with
whom she trusted shortly to unite in joy and
felicity; and seemed, as it were, to feel the
saying brought to pass, which is written, ' Death
is swallowed up in victory.' "

Read this, and be still.   Read this, and learn
that there is no weight of sorrow under which
genuine faith in GOD's word, cannot sustain you.

9. Make another comparison, I mean between your losses and trials, as a woman, and
your mercies and gains as a christian.   Here,
say you, is the grave of my dear husband,—
there, I say, is the cross, the grave, the throne
of your Redeemer.   Here, say you, is his vacant
seat at my table, his vacant place at my side,
his vacant chair at my hearth—there is GOD,
with his smiling countenance, his heart of love,
his covenant of grace, his all-sufficient resources,
to fill the vacuum.   Here, say you, is the weight
of woe and care pressing upon my heart, like a
dead unsupportable load—but there is *not* the

burden of unpardoned sin, sinking down your
soul to the bottomless pit. Here, say you, is
my now gloomy house—there is the house of
your GOD, always inhabited by his gracious
presence. Here, say you, I am a forlorn creature upon earth, having lost all that rendered
the world delightful—there is heaven glowing
like a brilliant firmament over your head, into
which your departed husband has entered, and
where you will soon join him in glory everlasting. Think how many widows there are, who
have no covenant GOD to go to ; no consolations
of the Spirit to sustain them; no pleasure in
the bible or in prayer to soothe them. You,
even you, ought to rejoice in a present Saviour
and a future heaven. All the attributes of GOD,
all the offices of CHRIST, all the consolations of
the Spirit, all the promises of scripture, all
the blessings of grace, all the prospects of glory
remain to be set over against your loss : and is
not this enough ?

D

# CHAPTER III.

## INSTRUCTION.

GOD is the best and only infallible teacher. " None teacheth like him." He delivereth his lessons in various ways, and through different mediums. The Scriptures, of course, contain the fullest and clearest revelation of his will; but these are corroborated and illustrated by the works of nature, and the dispensations of Providence. Events are pregnant with instruction. " Hence," saith the prophet, " the Lord's voice cometh unto the city ꝑ hear ye the rod, and who hath appointed it." Yes, every rod, as well as every word, has a voice; and it becomes us to listen to it. Afflicted woman, read the lessons which Providence has inscribed in dark characters on the tomb of your husband. It may be that GOD is saying to you, " I spake unto thee in thy prosperity, but thou saidst I will not hear ; this hath been thy manner from youth, that thou obeyedst not my voice."— Jer. xxii. 21.  Taken up with the enjoyment of the dear objects to be found in a quiet and comfortable home, you withheld your heart from God.  You neither loved, served, enjoyed, nor glorified him as the end of your existence.  Your husband was your idol, the stay and prop of your mind: and now God, who is a jealous God, and will not endure a rival, has removed the object of that supreme attachment, which ought to have been placed on *him;* and in language which derives additional weight and solemnity from being uttered over the sepulchre, saith " I am God, and there is none else.  Thou shalt have none other God besides me ; and thou shalt love the Lord thy God with all thy mind, and heart, and soul, and strength."  This is his demand now, and it always was.  It is not only what he says, now in the wilderness into which he has driven you, but what he said when you walked in the Eden of your earthly delight, and felt that your husband was to you as the tree of life in the midst

of the garden. Now then open your ear, and
hear the voice of his Providence. Open your
eye and read the lessons which, as I have said,
are inscribed on that tomb, which contains all
that was dearest to you on earth. Desire to
learn; be willing to learn; and much is needed
to be learnt from the sorrowful scenes through
which you have been, and still are called to
pass. When GOD takes such methods to teach,
surely you should be willing to learn; and it
may be that it is his intention to make up to
you by spiritual instruction and consolation, if
you will receive it, the loss he has called you to
sustain of temporal comfort.

1. Are you not most impressively reminded
of the evil of sin ?

What *could* more affectingly illustrate this,
than the deep sorrow which has fallen upon
you ? If the magnitude of an evil, may be as-
certained by the magnitude of its effects, what
must sin be, which has produced such consequences, as those you have witnessed. What
agonies it has inflicted, what ties it has rent
asunder, what desolation it has made, what

scenes it has produced, that widowed mother, those helpless, perhaps portionless babes, that gloomy house, those flowing tears too well proclaim! And what is the cause? Sin. "Sin entered into the world, and death by sin: so death hath passed upon all men, for that all have sinned." Yes; death with all its consequences, are the bitter fruits of sin. Had not man sinned he had been immortal. Every instance of death is the infliction of a penalty; for "the wages of sin is death." Think of what sin has robbed you. Calculate the mischief which it has wrought in your desolate abode. What has made you a widow? Sin. What has made your children fatherless? Sin. And think of the millions who are at this moment, in similar sad and melancholy circumstances. GOD is benevolent, and doth not afflict willingly, nor grieve the children of men; and yet he is perpetually multiplying widows and orphans by the ravages of death. How evil must sin be in his sight, when he takes this method of shewing his abhorrence of it; when he has fixed this penalty to it. And then this is only the *first* death, a mere type and symbol of that more painful "*second* death," which falleth upon the wicked in another world. Consider then the evil of sin. Take deep, large, views of it. Recollect *you* are a sinner: not vicious indeed, but virtuous; not profligate, but moral; but still a sinner in the sight of GOD. "For all have sinned and come short of the glory of GOD." Oh have you thought of this? Have you been convinced of sin by the Spirit of GOD? Have you *seen* your sinfulness, as well as heard of it? Felt it, as well as known it? Many have thought of their sins, for the first time in their life, with any seriousness, in their afflictions; and have said with the poet:—

Father! I bless thy gentle hand;
   How kind was thy chastising rod,
That brought my conscience to a stand,
   And brought my wandering soul to GOD.

Foolish and vain I went astray,
   E're I had felt thy scourges, Lord;
I lost my guide and lost my way:
   But now I love and keep thy word.

'Tis good to me to wear the yoke,
For pride is apt to rise and swell;
'Tis good to bear my Father's stroke,
That I might learn his statutes well.

If *you* have thought but little of sin till now,
may you begin to think upon it in your affliction. You have lost your husband, but how
much greater a calamity would be the loss of
your soul; and lost it must be, if you have no
just sense of sin. There can be no salvation
without pardon; and no pardon without repentance towards GOD, and faith in our Lord
JESUS CHRIST; and no repentance and faith,
without the knowledge of sin. Oh! what an
unutterable blessing will it prove; what a cause
for adoring wonder and gratitude through all
time and eternity too, if such affliction should
prove to be the means of your eternal salvation;
and if the death of the dear companion of your
life should be overruled for the salvation of your
immortal soul. Happy will it be, if led by this
event to think of the sinfulness of your heart
and conduct in the sight of GOD, you should be
brought, in the character of a true penitent,

and real believer, to the foot of the cross. How
will a sense of divine pardon sooth your sorrows! How will GOD's forgiving love comfort
your soul! How sweetly will you sing even
while the tear of widowhood is glittering in your
eye, and its sable costume is spread over you,
" It was good for me that I was afflicted."

2. Another lesson to be learnt by widowhood
is *the vanity of the world,* and its insufficiency
to make us happy. " Vanity of vanity, said the
preacher ; all is vanity, and vexation of spirit."
And you have found it to be so. You have
proved that the world, if not an unsatisfying,
is at any rate, an uncertain portion. How joy-
ous, till lately, were your circumstances. The
purest happiness of an earthly nature is that
which springs up in a comfortable home, where
there is a cordial union of hearts, as well as a
legal union of hands, between man and wife.
The tender sympathy, the delicate affection, the
minute attentions, the watchful solicitude, the
ceaseless offices of conjugal love, are the sweet-
est ingredient in the cup of life, and contribute
a thousand times more to terrestrial enjoyment,

than all the possessions of wealth, and all the blandishments of rank, station, and fashion. "With the affection, and health, and company of my husband," exclaims the fond and devoted wife, "I feel nothing wanting to my comfort, and can easily dispense with many things that others consider essential to their enjoyment." Such, perhaps, my mourning reader, was once your happy lot, for such a sharer of your domicile had you. Little cause had you to envy the gay or the great ; as little to sigh for their access to the party or the rout. To welcome at eventide, when the heat and burden of the day were over, the good man of the house, to his own fireside, and to your society, and to feel the honest pride and satisfaction of a wife, that *he* needed no other society to make him happy, this was your nightly joy, for years that flew too fast. Perhaps you thought too much had been said about the vanity of the world, for it was a pleasant world to *you*, and you were ready to blame the preacher, and call him ascetic and misanthropic, and reproach him for disturbing the happiness of others by the wailings of his own

disappointed heart.   But, ah! you too, have at
length returned an echo of that sad cry, and said
in the bitterness of your spirit, " All is vanity."
Yes, the lovely vision of your domestic bliss has
vanished.   Death has intruded, and changed
the scene.   No more returns at the accustomed
hour, the joy of your heart and the light of your
eyes.   His chair is vacant.   His place at the
fire-side, which knew him once, knows him no
more.   He is not on a journey.   No : he is in
the grave, and with him died the world to you.
Every thing is now changed; and you too exclaim, " Oh, vain world, thou hast deceived me.
Are all thy flattering smiles, and ample promises,
come to this ?   In one hour I have fallen from
the heights of happiness, into all the depths of
woe.   And am I a widow ?   Yes, and a widow
indeed."

*Such then is the world :* such all it can do to
make you happy.   Hearken to the language of
GOD, by the prophet, " My people have committed two evils, they have forsaken me, the fountain of living waters, and hewed them out cisterns,
broken cisterns, that can hold no water."   There

are the fragments of the broken cisterns; there
the spilled water; there the memorials of fragile
comfort, and disappointed hope;—and there,
hard by, let me add, the blessed contrast, the
full and flowing fountain, sending out its never
failing streams of pure and living waters. The
world has deceived and forsaken you. Now
turn to GOD. You cannot restore the broken
cistern, nor gather up the wasted contents : now
turn to the fountain. You have settled your
heart upon the creature, and it has proved a
quicksand; now settle it on GOD, " the rock of
ages." You have leaned upon an arm of flesh,
and it has failed you; now trust to the arms of
the Omnipotent Spirit. How many, when the
first shock of their disappointment was over, and
their faculties have recovered from the stunning
influence of their loss, have seen the folly as well
as sin, of trusting for happiness to mortal man,
and have turned their weeping, longing, and
imploring eye to the eternal GOD.

And even those who have been convinced
before, of the vanity of the world, at least by
profession, and have been taught to set their

hearts on God, have perhaps forgotten too much
their principles and their profession, and trusted
for a larger share of their happiness than they
ought to have done, to the things that are seen
and temporal. Yes, you who are called the
people of God, and are such, we hope, even you
have trusted far more to the world, to the life of
your husband, and to your other possessions
for your soul's portion, than was your duty.
An earthly-mindedness has crept over you and
damped the ardour of your religious affections.
You have sought the day-light of your soul
from the smile of a creature, instead of the
light of God's countenance; and now the lesser
luminary is extinguished, and you are in darkness. Still, however, the greater light remains;
the Sun of Righteousness is shining in all his
splendour and noon tide glory; go forth from
your gloomy and disconsolate situation into the
brightness and warmth of his heart cheering
radiance, and sun yourself in the ardor of his
beams.

3. What a lesson does widowhood teach of
the power and value of true religion : and that

in two ways. First by the influence of it, where
it is possessed, in supporting the mind and consoling it, amidst sorrows which from any other
source, knows not consolation's name. I appeal
to devout and holy women, who have been enabled in the hour of their extremity to cast
themselves by faith, and prayer, and submission upon God, and to still the tumult of their
thoughts, and keep down the rising tide of their
grief, by the potency of his grace, whether the
value of piety ever rose so high in their esteem,
as in that moment when they first answered to
the name of widow, and they felt that they could
do it without fainting at the sound. Friends
gathered round them in all the tenderness of
sympathy, and there was a balm in their words,
and looks, and actions; but at the same time,
each new comer seemed in other respects to
open their wounds afresh, and to be a new re-
membrancer of the loss sustained. It was only
when the mourner could get to her bible, and
to her God, in all the power of faith and prayer,
that she felt she could be sustained; and then
she *did* feel it. Astonished at her own calm-

ness; at her tranquillity amidst such a wreck, she at first questioned whether it was indifference, stupefaction, or religion. It could not be the first, for she was as sure of her love, as she was sure of her existence; nor the second, for she reasoned, reflected, and anticipated; it must therefore, she said, be the last; it must be faith laying hold of the promise, and staying itself in darkness upon the name of GOD. It must be the power of GOD perfecting its might in weakness: the flowing in of grace into a soul, which grace has first made willing and able to receive it. How wondrous must the faith of ABRAHAM have appeared to himself, when he came to reflect on what he had done, or rather what the grace of GOD had wrought in him, in his willingness to offer up ISAAC. Inferior to this, of course, but analagous to it, has been the surprise of many an afflicted widow at the submission and confidence with which she laid the ashes of her husband in the sepulchre. What else could have so sustained her, bereft as she was of what gave to earth its chief interest? Let that religion still support you. What it has done, it can do. It has proved to you its reality and its power: still trust it as the anchor of your soul, sure and stedfast. If it prevented you from sinking, when the shock came first upon you, it can do the same through every future stage of your solitary journeying, and every future scene of your now unshared sorrow.

But perhaps your present situation demonstrates the excellency of religion, by another medium of proof, I mean by the want of it. You have *not* religion to support you, and you have therefore literally nothing. The storm has come, and you are without a shelter. The cup of wormwood and gall is put into your hand, and you have nothing with which to sweeten it. Well then now, when every thing else fails, turn to this one and only refuge that remains. It opens to you now. You feel that nothing else is of any avail. It is not too late. God waits to be gracious. Oh let me now sound in your ears the music of our Lord's comfortable words, " Come unto me, all ye that labour and are heavy laden, and I will give you rest." Oh

mark that, *the heavy laden*. No matter what
may be the burden, whether of sin, or of care,
or of sorrow, there is rest from it in CHRIST.
If you look to him by faith to take away the
burden of your sin, he will lighten every other
load that presses upon your spirit. JESUS
CHRIST, the Saviour of the lost, is the comforter
of the distressed. He meets the natural cry of
misery, and goes out to wipe away the tears of
sorrow, by the hand of his redeeming mercy.
He came to bind up the broken-hearted, and to
comfort those that mourn : but it is in his own
way. Many have come to him, led as it seemed
by the mere instinctive longing after happiness,
and have tried faith in the gospel as a last and
almost hopeless experiment, after the failure of
every other attempt to obtain consolation. And
oh ! what an unlooked for discovery have they
made ; they who had found no resting place in
the world, and who had wandered through it in
quest of some object however insignificant, that
might divert them from their sorrows, and for
a moment at least remove the sense of that hopeless grief which lay dead upon the heart, found

now an object which the widest desires of their
soul could not grasp, and of such irresistible
power as to turn the current of their feelings, I
mean the salvation which is in CHRIST JESUS,
with eternal glory. They who had been ready to
abandon life, as having no charm, and to embrace
death as having no greater terror than their
present affliction, now see that even in the ab-
scence of that which once threw over their existence its deepest interest, they can find something
worth living for, in the pursuit of an eternal
joy. While in sorrow and in desolation they
went to JESUS for comfort, the Spirit, whose
secret, but unknown influence guided their steps,
opened the eyes of their understanding to discern the path of life, and by the aid of a hope
full of immortality, to rise above the ravages of
death, and the spoliations of the grave. Thus
while like MARY MAGDALENE, they were lingering round the sepulchre, the Saviour revealed
himself to them, and they dried up their tears
in the presence of their Lord. May it be so
with those who shall read these pages. May
you in your affliction turn to religon, that grand

E

catholicon, and panacea, for the sorrows of life.
You do not know, even yet, how much you will
need it, in the future stages of your sad and
solitary journey.   The friends whom the fresh-
ness of your grief has gathered round you, may
forget your loss much sooner than you will; and
the force of their sympathy may have spent itself,
long before the tide of your grief has ceased to
flow.   Few, very few, are the faithful friends
whose tender interest is as long lived and as deep
as our tribulation.   Sympathy wears out long
before that which calls it into existence : and
then, what can comfort you but religion ?   Venture not forward, without decided and fervent
piety.   Let your next step be from the tomb of
a husband, to the cross of a Saviour.

Take the following instance as at once a
direction and an encouragement :—

In the course of my pastoral walks among my
flock, I one day called upon a young widow, who
has become a member of the church under my
care since the death of her husband.   I found
her at her mangle, by which, and by letting a
room or two to lodgers, she earns a scanty and

precarious support for herself and child. I found her somewhat indisposed, exhausted by labour, and depressed, though not desponding, in consequence of her lodgings being unoccupied, and her work rather short. I entered into conversation with her on her necessitous and afflictive circumstances, when she expressed her strong confidence in GOD, and her expectation she should be provided for. She soon reverted to her husband, who had been a consistent member of my flock. Her eulogy upon his memory was in strong and tender language. She described him as having been one of the kindest and most indulgent of husbands, and implied that she had of course been a happy wife :— " But," said she, " *I can thank the Lord for his death, for in consequence of that sad event, I now hope to be associated with him, in the presence of Christ in heaven.*" The fact is, the death of her husband was the painful means, in the hands of the Spirit, of her saving conversion to GOD. In this you see one instance among many in which widowhood has been the furnace of affliction, where GOD has chosen some of his people, and

E 2

called them to pass through the fiery trial to bring them to himself. The female whose case I am now narrating, by the piety she then obtained, and by the sweet hope of meeting her deceased husband in the land where there shall be no more death, endures with a sorrowful cheerfulness the desolation of widowhood and the rigours of poverty.

What lessons does this little incident teach ! What a potency and a heavenly balm are there in true religion ; what present and what future advantages does it yield, when it can enable a poor widow, to bow with her fatherless child at the grave of her departed husband, or in the dreary abode once made happy by his presence and his love, and give GOD thanks for his removal, because of the eternal felicity that would result to both in heaven, from their early separation upon earth ! What an admonition to those who like this poor woman have lost pious husbands, while they themselves are not yet partakers of true experimental piety. Let them consider the reasoning which is implied in her gratitude,—" Had my husband lived, I should have been content with my happiness as a wife, and have sought none from a higher source, and perhaps have lived and died a stranger to true religion. Thus after enjoying his society a few years upon earth, I should have been banished not only from his company but from the presence of the Lord for ever: but now since his death was sanctified for my conversion to GOD, I have lost him for a season, to be with him for ever in glory." O widow, whose husband has left you as did hers, in an unconverted state, let it be your desire, your prayer, your resolution to turn this deep affliction to your soul's advantage. You have lost his life; lose not also his death. He bends to you from the skies, and with accents of faithful love, says to you, "Follow me to heaven. Let us not be separated for ever. Let faith, prayer, and submission, heal the wound of separation. O let us meet in the blessed world of life and joy." Comply with the admonition, and then you too will be able to comprehend the thanksgiving of this poor woman for the decease of a loving husband.

And now take the testimony of another

widow who related in the following language her
sad, yet in another view of it, her happy experience, to a minister who visited her :—

"My husband died, and then disease seized
on my children, and they were taken one by one.
In the course of a few years, I had lain those in
whom my heart was bound up, in the grave.
Oh! they were many, many bitter tears that I
shed. The world was dark. The very voice of
consolation was a pain. I could sit by the side
of my friend, but could not hear him speak of
my departed ones. My affliction was too deep
to be shared. It seemed as if GOD himself had
deserted me. I was alone. The places at the
table and the fire-side remained—but they who
filled them were gone. Oh the loneliness, as it
had been a tomb, of my chamber. How blessed
was sleep! For then the dead lived again.
They were all around me. My youngest child
and last, sat on my knee—she leaped up in my
arms, she uttered my name with infant joyous-
ness; and that sweet tone was as if an angel
had spoken to my sad soul. But the dream
vanished, and the dreary morning broke, and I

waked, and prayed, and I sought forgiveness, even while I uttered it for my unholy prayer —prayed that GOD would let me lie down in the grave side by side with my children and husband.

"But better thoughts came. In my grief I remembered that though my loved ones were separated from me, the same Father—the same Infinite Love, watched over them as when they were by my fire-side. We were divided, but only for a season. And by degrees, my grief grew calmer. But since then, my thoughts have been more in that world, where they have gone, than in this. I do not remember less, but I look forward and upward more. I learned the worth of prayer and reliance. Would that I could express to every mourner how the sting is taken away from the grief of one, who with a true and full heart puts her trust in GOD. I can never again go into the gay world. The pleasures of this world are no longer pleasures to me. But I have trust, and hope, and confidence. I know that my Redeemer liveth. I know that GOD ever watches over his children. And in my desolation, this faith of the heart has long enabled me to feel a different kind of pleasure indeed, but a far deeper, though more sober joy, than the pleasures of this world ever gave me even when youth, and health, and friends all conspired to give them their keenest relish.

" 'You have learned in your own heart,' I said, 'that all trials are not evils.'

" It was with eyes up-turned to heaven, and gushing over with tears, not tears of sorrow, but gratitude, and with a radiant countenance, that she answered, in a tone so mild, so rapt, as if her heart were speaking to her God,—' It has been good for me that I have been afflicted.' "

4. What an impressive view does your affliction give you of the solemnity of death, and the necessity of being prepared for it.   You have now not only heard of the awful visitor, or read of him, but you have seen him : and though his icy hand has not been laid on *you*, it has taken from your side the companion of your life.   It is not a book, a sermon, a preacher, but death himself that has spoken to you, who as he bore away the dear object of your affection, looked

back unpityingly, and sternly said, "I come for you soon." He will. Listen also to the voice of one who with milder accents than those of the last enemy, says to you, "Be ye also ready, for at such an hour as ye think not, the Son of Man cometh." Can you ever forget the scene? The dread reality? The harbingers, the concomitants, the consequences of dissolution? The pain, the sickness, the restlessness, the delirium, the torpor—and then the mortal stillness which ten thousand thunders could not disturb? Oh what a change is death! Is that the time, that the scene, those the circumstances, to which it is wise and safe to defer the business of religion, the concerns of the soul, the pursuit of salvation? You saw how all but insupportable were the last woes of expiring nature; or how sudden was the stroke; or how shattered was the reason; and how impossible it was *then* to meditate on matters which require the concentrated attention, the calm undisturbed possession of all the faculties of the soul. Learn then a lesson from that scene never to be forgotten, and instantly to be practiced, of being prepared at

once, and completely, for the great change. You
saw how valueless in death is every thing but
salvation, and how all but impossible it is to
commence the momentous concern then. Be
wise then, and consider your own latter end.
Preparation for death is living work. A life of
faith, holiness, and devotion is the only preparation for a death-bed. Be this one of the bene-
ficial results of losing an object so dear. On
his tomb, devote yourself to the pursuit of salvation, as the business of life, and the only
suitable meetness for death.

It is said with equal power and beauty by a
well known and deservedly admired living writer,
" I consider the scene of death, as being to the
interested parties, who witness it, a kind of
*sacrament,* inconceivably solemn, at which they
are summoned by the voice of heaven to pledge
themselves in vows of irreversible decision.
Here then, as at the high altar of eternity, *you*
have been called to pronounce, if I may so express it, the inviolable oath, to keep for ever in
view, the momentous value of life, and to aim
at its worthiest use, its sublime end—to spurn,

with lasting disdain, those foolish trifles, those fri-
volous vanities, which so generally wither in our
sight, and consume life as the locusts did Egypt ;
and to devote yourself with the ardor of passion,
to attain the most divine improvement of the
human soul ; and in short, to hold yourself in
preparation to make that interesting transition
to another life, whenever you shall be claimed
by the LORD of the world."

# CHAPTER IV.

———

## CONSOLATION.

Yes! consolation. Yours, even yours is not a case that excludes all comfort. There is balm for the wounds of a widow's heart.

1. It may seem a strange and unlikely method of comforting you, to remind you of happiness for ever fled, and scenes of enjoyment that have vanished like some bright vision; but is it not a comfort to retrace the history of your union, and to remember that you loved and were beloved; that you lived in harmony and peace with your departed husband; that you had his confidence and his heart, and he yours; that you travelled pleasantly together in this desert world, and made the journey a delightful one while it lasted? You have nothing but holy and happy reminiscences. Is not this better than the retrospect of an ill-assorted match,

and the scenes of discord and strife which such unions bring with them? His picture, his chair, his dear name, if they form the most sorrowful, yet, at the same time, do they awaken the most sacred associations. His image, as it rises in the region of imagination, is no sullen spectre, cold, frowning, and perturbed, and that looks upon you as if to upbraid you for the past; but it is a blessed shade, smiling, complacent, and calm, that still beams with the same affection with which it was wont to do: and you feel as if you had nothing to offer in the way of apology or atonement, for the purpose of propitiating and tranquillising it. You still feel in mysterious and happy fellowship, though separated by the wide deep gulph of the grave. Extract comfort, then, from your very tears, for love has left a drop even in *them*. You were happy, and that should prevent you being wretched now: you were his comfort on earth, and assisted him on his pilgrimage to heaven; where, perhaps, he is now thinking of you before the throne, and finding a place for your name in the song of his gratitude before the fountain of mercy.

2. Perhaps you were permitted to be with him in his mortal sickness, and to minister to his comfort, as long as he needed it and was capable of understanding your ministrations. "I am glad I am not a king," said a dying husband to an affectionate and devoted wife, who never left him night or day, till his spirit forsook its clay: "for then," continued he, "I should not be waited upon by *you*." How tender and how soothing are the attentions of a wife at all times; but oh what are they *not* in the chamber of sickness and death. Men who set little value on the kind offices of their wives in the time of health and activity, have been glad to have them at their bed-side, in the season of disease, and at the last hour: but how doubly precious are such offices in death, to those who loved their wives, and prized their attentions in life. Such, afflicted woman, was, perhaps, your case. You were his constant attendant. You waited, watched and laboured, to the uttermost of your strength, to smooth the pillow of sickness, and the bed of death. The food, and the medicine were always most wel-

come from your gentle hand; he forgot his
pains in your presence; and it was some miti-
gation of her sorrows, while as his ministering
angel you occupied the post of observation,
darker every hour, that you saw how much you
contributed to his comfort. You heard the
words of love and gratitude that fell from the
sufferer's lips; you saw the looks and tears which
spoke what words were too weak to utter; and
taxed your energies almost beyond what nature
could supply, to meet the necessities of one
whose flickering lamp seemed to be kept from
extinction, by your vigilance and tenderness.

Well, it is all over now. Affection has done
its last, as well as its best, and its uttermost. Is
it not consoling to you to think of all this?—
Especially if you were enabled to minister to the
comfort of the soul, as well as to the body, and
by words of scripture promise, to drive away
the gloomy thoughts and disturbing fears which
lighted upon his spirit as he approached the
dark valley. Perhaps it was reserved for that
solemn hour, for your dying husband to disclose
to you the state of his soul, and to express to

your more entire satisfaction, than you had felt before, his sense of sin, his faith in Christ, and his hope of glory. How beautifully is this described in the life of Mrs. GRAHAM, of New York. "He brought me, and my idol," says that excellent woman, "out of a barren land, placed us under the breath of prayer, among a dear little society of methodists; he laid us upon their spirits, and when the messenger, death, was sent for my beloved, the breath of prayer ascended from his bedside, from their little meeting; and I believe from their families and closets. The God of mercy prepared their hearts to pray, and his ear to hear, and the answers did not tarry. Behold, my husband prayeth; confesses sin; applies to the Saviour; pleads for forgiveness for his sake; receives comfort; blesses GOD for JESUS CHRIST, and dies with these words upon his tongue, 'I hold fast by the Saviour.' Behold another wonder! the idolatress in an ecstasy of joy. She who never could realise a separation for one single minute during his life, now resigns her heart's treasure, with praise and thanksgiving. O the joy of that hour! its savour remains in my heart to this moment. For five days and nights, I had been little off my knees, it was my ordinary posture at his bed-side, and in all that time, I had but *once* requested his life. The Spirit helped my infirmities with groanings that could not be uttered, leading me to pray for that which GOD had determined to bestow; making intercession for my husband according to the will of GOD."

3. And this is intimately connected with another source of consolation, I mean the consideration of the happiness of your departed sainted husband, where indeed there is satisfactory ground to believe he died in the LORD. "How does the reflection," said Mrs. HUNTINGDON, after she became a widow, "that our departed friends have reached the point which we must reach before we can be happy, sweeten and soothe the anguish of separation! Let us contemplate them in every supposeable view, and the prospect is full of consolation. We cannot think of them as what they were, or what they are, without pleasure. They are the highly

F

favoured of the LORD, who, having finished all
that they had to do in this vale of tears, are
admitted to the higher services of the upper
temple. True, when we look at our loss, nature
will feel." Be it so, that you are sorrowful, it
is not, as regards your husband, a sorrow without hope. You have no grief on his account.
Time was when you wept for *him :* you saw him
burdened with care; exhausted by labour; perplexed with difficulties; sometimes humbled by
a sense of his imperfections; and in his closing
scenes, pale with sickness, racked with pain,
till the tears glistened in his eye, and the groan
escaped his breast; but he will suffer no more;
the days of his mourning are ended; and he is
floating on a fullness of joy in GOD's presence,
and surrounded with pleasures for evermore at
his right hand. Strive then so far to rise above
your grief, as to rejoice with him, though he
cannot weep with you. You loved, and tried to
make him happy upon earth, and smiled when
you in any measure succeeded; take some
comfort in the thought that GOD has made him
happy in heaven. Think of him not as in the

grave, but as in glory. Say in the language of that beautiful epitaph,

Forgive, blest shade ! the tributary tear,
   That mourns thy exit from a world like this,
Forgive the wish, that would have kept thee here,
   And stayed thy progress to the seats of bliss.

No more confin'd to grovelling scenes of night,
   No more a tenant pent in mortal clay,
Now should we rather hail thy glorious flight,
   And trace thy journey to the realms of day.

But perhaps, in all this, I do but lacerate some widows' heart already wounded, by the fear, their husbands' spirits are not in heaven. Then turn from the subject in deep and silent submission. Confide in the equity of GOD. Rely upon his unerring wisdom. If you cannot reflect with comfort, and hope, endeavour not to reflect at all. Say, " shall not the judge of all the earth do right ?" If this source of consolation be closed, turn to the others, and they are many.

4. Recollect that GOD lives. " He lives, said the Psalmist, "and blessed be my rock,

F 2

and let the GOD of my salvation be exalted."
GOD lives! What a compass of thought and
of consolation is there in that one expression;
and akin to it is the language of CHRIST, to the
beloved apostle in the isle of Patmos, " Behold,
I am alive for evermore." Die who will, CHRIST
lives. How often is he called in scripture, "THE
LIVING GOD;" it is one of his most frequently
repeated titles; and dwelling as we do, amidst
the tombs, it is one of his most comforting, as
well as one of his most sublime and impressive
ones, especially to those who have been called
to sustain the loss of friends by death. Thus
we find there is a title, and attribute, and view,
and operation of GOD, suited to all the varieties
of our circumstances, our wants, our woes, and
our fears. There is bounty for our wants;
mercy for our sins and miseries; patience for
our provocations; power for our weakness;
truth for our fears; wisdom for our ignorance;
immutability for our vicissitudes; and because
our friends are dying, and we also are following
them to the grave, he is presented to us as the
*living* GOD. And as he lives, all that belongs

to him lives with him. His attributes neither change nor die. Just look at one view of his nature and conduct as given by the apostle : *" The God of all comfort."*—2 Cor. i. 3." Beautiful representation ! And akin to it is that other, " GOD that comforteth those that are cast down."—2 Cor. vii. 7. What ideas are contained in these two aspects of GOD. They seem to tell us that not only is all comfort in him, and from him, and for all people who are willing to be comforted ; not only that his consolations are such as by way of eminence and excellence, deserve to be called comfort, almost exclusively; but also that he is in his nature *all* comfort to his people, and in his dealings *always* comforting them. His nature is one vast fountain of consolation, and his operations, so many streams flowing from it. Now this GOD lives ; lives to comfort *you.* Your earthly comforter is gone ; but your heavenly one remains. Is there not enough in his power to protect and support you; in his wisdom to guide you; in his all sufficiency to provide for you ; in his goodness to pity you ; in his love to supply you; in his presence

to cheer you? In your troubled and broken
condition of mind, you need subjects of consolation which are not only sufficient in themselves,
but which can be simply expressed and easily
apprehended, without any long train of thought,
or elaboration of argument. Here then is one,
containing all comforts *in* one, *" God lives."*
Seize the simple yet wondrous conception; take
it home to your afflicted bosom; apply it to your
forlorn and desolate spirit; repeat it to yourself;
and by the power of it drive away unbelief, dis-
trust, and all the crowd of dark, desponding
thoughts, which hover like foul birds of night
over the desolate heart, there to nestle, and
utter their moaning voices. Learn from a little
child who seeing her widowed mother in weeds
and in tears, asked the question, " Is GOD Almighty dead, Mamma!"

5. The Lord JESUS CHRIST in all his mediatorial offices, all his redeeming grace, all his
tender sympathy, and all the blessings of his
salvation, still remains. " Fear not," said he
to JOHN, in language already quoted, " I am
the first and the last. I am he that liveth, and

was dead; and behold I am alive for evermore, and have the keys of hell, (the unseen world) and of death."—Rev. i. 19. Oh there is enough in these sublime words to support and comfort all the widows that are at this moment, or ever will be upon earth. Here they are not only told, that the Redeemer has exclusive dominion over death and the invisible world, so that none ever turns, or holds the key but himself, but also that he lives in all the plenitude of his power and grace to comfort those that survive. All that there is in the incarnation and death of CHRIST as the Saviour of a lost and ruined world; in his resurrection from the grave; in his ascension into heaven, and intercession at the right hand of the Father; in his universal government of the world; in the promise, the purpose, and the hope of his second coming; in the assurance that he is now in the midst of his church, and will never leave it; in the distant prospect of the millennial days when his glory shall cover all lands;—all this remains to console the hearts of his mourning people in their sorrows upon earth, and connected with all this, are the blessings that result from his mediatorial work, the pardon of all our sins, the justification of our persons, the sanctification of our nature, adoption, perseverance;—in short a perfect salvation. And is there one who can think so little of these things as to find in them no adequate consolation in the hour and scene of her woe! Oh believer, is there not enough in *all this,* to save you from fainting? Bereaved woman, shall your sorrows at the grave of the most affectionate husband that a wife ever had, or ever lost, weigh down the cross, the atonement, the righteousness, the sympathy, the grace of CHRIST? He is still the same as to compassion, as he was when upon earth. Those eyes that wept at the grave of LAZARUS, look on you; that bosom that groaned over the sorrows of MARTHA and MARY, cherishes you. He that pitied the widow of Nain, pities you. " In all your affliction, he is afflicted, and the angel of his presence is with you." In all his unsearchable riches of grace, in his promises of truth, and in his invitations he is with you, and has said, " I will never leave thee, nor forsake thee. Not a promise died, when your husband did; not a fruit of grace, or an an earnest of glory withered when he departed. Not a single gospel consolation lies entombed in his sepulchre. The cup of your earthly prosperity may be emptied, but not a drop is lost from the cup of salvation. Death has deprived you of your temporal enjoyment, but your eternal salvation in CHRIST still remains. You are called to bear *your* cross, but look up, there is CHRIST bearing, and borne by, his also. In one sense your husband sleeps in the tomb of JESUS; for we " are dead and buried with him." Wherefore comfort yourself with these thoughts.

5. *God has in a most especial manner interested himself on behalf of widows, and their fatherless children.*

Just see how he has literally crowded the page of inspiration, with declarations concerning them. He has revealed himself in a very especial manner as the widow's GOD.

Observe how he has fenced in their interests and protected them from injury. " Ye shall not afflict any widow or fatherless child."—

Exod. xxii. 22. "Thou shalt not take the widow's garment to pledge."—Deut. xxiv. 17. "Cursed be he that perverteth the judgment of the fatherless and the widow."—Deut. xxix. 19. "Judge the fatherless, plead for the widow."—Isaiah i. 17. "If ye oppress the fatherless and the widow, then will I cause you to dwell in this place."—Jer. iii. 6. "Oppress not the widow, nor the fatherless."—Zech. vii. 10. "In this have they vexed the widow."—Ezek. xxii. 7.

Observe next the injunctions delivered not even to neglect the widow. "And the fatherless and the widow which are within thy gates, shall come, and shall eat, and shall be satisfied, that the Lord thy GOD may bless thee in all the work of thy hand, that thou doest."—Deut. xiv. 29. "When thou hast made an end of tithing all the tithes of thine increase the third year, which is the year of tithing, and hast given it unto the Levite, the stranger, the fatherless, and the widow, that they may eat within thy gates, and be filled; then thou shalt say before the Lord thy GOD, I have brought away the hallowed things out of mine house, and also have given them unto the Levite, and unto the stranger, to the fatherless, and to the widow, according to all the commandments which thou hast commanded me : I have not transgressed thy commandments, neither have I forgotten them."—Deut. xxvi. 12, 13.

Then dwell upon those passages in which kindness to widows is spoken of by men, or by GOD himself. "I caused the widow's heart to sing for joy."—Job xxvi. 13. In opposition to which he gives it as the mark of the wicked; "They drive away the ass of the fatherless, and take the widow's ox for a pledge."—Job xxiv. 3. "The Lord will establish the border of the widow."—Prov. xv. 25. "A judge of the fatherless and widows is GOD in his holy habitation."—Psalm lxix. 5. "Leave thy fatherless children, I will preserve them alive, and let thy widows trust in me."—Jer. xlix. 11. "Pure religion and undefiled before GOD and the Father is this,—to visit the fatherless and widows in their affliction."—James i. 27.

What widow is there who in casting her eye over such passages as these, but must be com-

forted in thus witnessing the deep interest God
takes in her forlorn condition, when he has not
only promised her what he will do himself, but
commanded in every variety of form and expression all others to sympathise with her, and ac-
tually to befriend her.    She may surely say:—

> Poor though I am, despised, forgot,
> Yet God, my God ! forsakes me not.

Whoever is passed over by Jehovah, the widow
receives his special notice.

6. Perhaps you have still many friends left ;
for it is rarely the case that a widow has none,
either on her own side, or on that of her late
husband.    There is something in your case that
calls forth sympathy.    Your very dress with
silent but expressive signs, seems to say, " My
husband is in his grave, pity me."    Hearts not
easily moved have relented, and eyes unaccustomed to weep have shed tears, at the recital
of your loss.    Low as human nature has sunk
by our apostacy from God, it has not lost all
that is kind and amiable towards our fellow-
creatures, and in the exercise of this kindness,

CONSOLATION. **77**

many are predisposed to be the friends of the widow. Do not refuse their friendship. Open your hearts and let them pour in the balm of sympathy. Do not discourage them in their efforts to interest or please, nor undervalue them. The sun of your bright day has set, and it is night: but do not despise the lunar beams, nor even the twinkling of a few scattered stars: even this is better than rayless gloom. Some, I admit there are, who in losing their husband, lose almost every friend they have on earth. Let them think of the friend, who is all friends in one, I mean, the widow's GOD.

7. Is there not upon record such an assurance as this, "All things work together for good to them that love GOD, to them that are the called according to his promise."—Rom. viii. 28. The consolation I know is limited to a particular class of persons, "to them that love GOD and are called according to his purpose," and none have a right to appropriate the comfort, but they who answer to the character. To none else can good come out of evil: for none else is GOD preparing a happy result of all their trou-

bles; for none else are his mighty and glorious
attributes of wisdom and power weaving the
dark threads of their history into a texture of
felicity, and a garment of praise. But then all
are invited, and may instantly accept the invitation, to come within the comprehension of
this circle of good, by coming through faith into
the love of GOD. To those who are already
there, how inexpressibly consoling, if they have
faith to receive it, is the assurance, that there
is good to be extracted for the widow, from her
tears. Observe it is *good*, not *ease :* concealed,
not apparent good; future, not present good.
What an illustration of this passage of scripture is the history of the patriarch JOSEPH.
Sorrow upon sorrow settled on the heart of his
venerable father, as one bad report of his children after another fell upon his ear, till in the
agony of his spirit he exclaimed, "All these
things are against me." And judging by appearances, he was right. Appearances, however were fallacious. JACOB could not see to
the end, and he who cannot, should not pronounce what the end will be. All things were at

the time working together for good, though it was impossible for him to conjecture in what way. Equally impossible is it for you to see, or even to imagine, nor do I pretend to foretel, in what way good can rise to you from a husband's grave. All your brightest prospects have vanished; all your springs of earthly consolation are dried up; your support and that of your children, is cut off; in such an event, reason can see nothing but unmixed evil for the present, and portents of woe for the future; and it really seems like a mockery of your woe to tell you, it will work for your good. But is it not promised? If so, it must be fulfilled, though in a way unknown to us. Suppose any one had gone to the venerable patriarch when he was weeping, first for Joseph, and then for Benjamin, and uttered this astonishing language in his hearing, "All is working for your good;" would he not have looked up, and with a reproving voice, said, "Do you come to mock me?" Yet he lived to see that it was so. If God says it is good, it must be so, for he can *make* it good. It may

not be good for your temporal comfort, but it
may be for your eternal welfare; and if not for
yours, it may be for your children's; if not for
theirs, it may have been for your husband's.
You may never see how it is for good in this
world.   Many go all their lives without having
the mystic characters of the event decyphered,
and the secret workings of God's love laid
open; they die in ignorance of his plans, though
not of his purposes.   So it may be with you.
The right side of the embroidery may never be
turned to you here, and looking only at the
tangled threads and dark colours of the back
part, all now appears confusion; but when the
front view shall be seen, and the design of the
divine artist, and all the connexions of the piece
shall be pointed out, and the colouring shall be
shewn in the light of heaven, with what adoring
wonder, delight, and gratitude will you exclaim,
as the whole bursts upon your sight, " O the
depth of the riches of the wisdom and knowledge of God!   How unsearchable are his
judgments, and his ways past finding out.   All
things have worked together for my good."

8. Recollect the admonition of the apostle ; "This I say, brethren, the time is short : it remaineth, that both they that have wives, be as though they had none ; and they that weep, as though they wept not ; and they that rejoice, as though they rejoiced not ; and they that use the world, as not abusing it ; for the fashion of this world passeth away."—1 Cor. vii. 29-31. *Time is short.* Solemn expression ! ˉThe death of the worldling's joy ; but the solace of the christian's sorrows. Widow, you cannot weep long, even though you go weeping to your grave. The days of your mourning are numbered, and must end soon. The vale of tears is not interminable. You are passing through it ; and will soon pass out of it. Be patient, the coming of the Lord draweth nigh. Eternity is at hand, through the everlasting ages of which you will weep no more, for GOD shall wipe away all tears from the eyes of his people. In hell sinners weep for ever ; in heaven saints never weep.

9. And then what felicity awaits you on that blessed shore, on which your departed husband

G

stands looking back wonderingly on the dark waters of the river he has passed, and beckoning you away to the realms of immortality. You will soon follow to the regions of which it is said, "there will be no more death." Heaven is *a world of life,* eternal life, never to be interrupted by the entrance, or even the fear of death : and this is before you. They who are united by the bonds of christian, as well as conjugal love, do not lose one another in the dark valley never to meet in the world of immortals. They drop the fleshly bond in the grave, and all that appertained to it, but not the spiritual tie that makes them one in CHRIST. United in the honors and felicities of that blessed world, where *all* are blessed perfectly, and for ever, you shall receive together the answer of those prayers you presented upon earth ; realise the anticipations you indulged while travelling across the desert of mortality ; trace together the providential events of your earthly history ; learn why you were united, and why separated ; see the wisdom and goodness of those events, which once appeared so dark, and drew so many tears from

your eyes; indulge in reminiscences, all of
which will furnish new occasions of wonder, new
motives to praise, and new sources of delight;
point one another to the vista of everlasting ages
opening before you, through which an endless
succession of joys are advancing to meet you;
and then, filled with a pure, unearthly love for
each other, fall down before the throne of the
Lamb, and feel every other affection absorbed in
supreme, adoring love to him.   Such a scene is
before you; and if it be, then bear your sorrows,
afflicted woman, for in what felicities are they
to issue, and how soon!

But, perhaps, I should help to comfort the
mourner, if, in addition to those gracious promises and directions which are specially appropriate to the case of widows, and which have
been already presented to your notice, I lay
before you a selection of passages of scripture,
which are applicable to all persons in trouble.
What words may be expected to have such
power over the sorrowful heart, as those of GOD.
Many of these have been already quoted, but
there may be an advantage in bringing them all
together in one view before the mind.

### GOD'S END IN AFFLICTING.

For thou, oh GOD, hast proved us: thou hast tried us, as silver is tried.—Psalm lxvi. 10.

Furthermore we have had fathers of our flesh which corrected us, and we gave them reverence: shall we not much rather be in subjection unto the Father of spirits, and live? For they verily for a few days chastened us after their own pleasure; but he for our profit, that we might be partakers of his holiness.—Heb. xii. 9, 10.

### GOD'S JUSTICE AND FAITHFULNESS IN OUR TRIALS.

Righteous art thou, O Lord, when I plead with thee.—Jer. xii. 1.

He hath not dealt with us after our sins, nor rewarded us according to our iniquities.—Psalm ciii. 10.

It is of the Lord's mercies we are not consumed.—Lam. iii. 22.

Wherefore doth a living man complain, a man for the punishment of his sins?—Lam. iii. 39.

I will bear the indignation of the Lord, because I have sinned against him.—Micah vii. 9.

I know, O Lord, that in faithfulness thou hast afflicted me.—Psalm cxix. 75.

### GOD'S LOVE IN AFFLICTING US.

My son, despise not thou the chastening of the Lord; neither be weary of his correction: for whom the Lord loveth he correcteth, even as a father doth the son, in whom he delighteth. —Prov. iii. 11, 12.

For whom the Lord loveth he chasteneth, and scourgeth every son whom he receiveth.— Heb. xii. 6.

As many as I love, I rebuke and chasten.— Rev. iii. 19.

### GOD A COMFORTER.

The GOD of all comfort, who comforteth us in all our tribulation.—2 Cor. i. 3.

GOD that comforteth those that are cast down. —2 Cor. vii. 6.

### GOD A REFUGE.

GOD is our refuge and strength, a very present help in time of trouble. The Lord of

Hosts is with us, the GOD of JACOB is our refuge.—Psalm xlvi. 1.

### GOD'S PRESENCE WITH US IN THE DEEPEST TRIBULATION.

When thou passest through the waters I will be with thee ; and through the rivers they shall not overflow thee; when thou walkest through the fire, thou shalt not be burned, neither shall the flame kindle upon thee.—Isaiah xliii. 2.

### GOD'S EYE UPON HIS PEOPLE IN SORROW.

He knoweth the way that I take, when he has tried me I shall come forth as gold.—Job xxiii. 10.

### GOD CANNOT FORGET HIS PEOPLE.

Can a woman forget her sucking child, that she should not have compassion on the son of her womb ? Yea, she may forget, yet will I not forget thee.—Isaiah xlix. 15.

### TRUST IN GOD ENJOINED, ENCOURAGED, AND EXEMPLIFIED.

And they that know thy name, will put their

trust in thee, for thou hast not forsaken them that seek thee.—Psalm ix. 10.

And now Lord, what wait I for, my hope is in thee.—Psalm xxxix. 7.

Thou wilt keep him in perfect peace, whose mind is stayed on thee, because he trusteth in thee.   Trust ye in the Lord for ever; for in the Lord Jehovah is everlasting strength.—Isaiah xxvi. 3-4.

Though he slay me, yet will I trust in him. —Job xiii. 15.

### CONSOLATORY ASSURANCES.

Affliction cometh not forth of the dust, neither doth trouble spring out of the ground.   Job v. 6.

They that seek the Lord shall not want any good thing.—Psalm xxxiv. 10.

Trust in the Lord and do good, so shalt thou dwell in the land, and verily thou shalt be fed. —Psalm xxxvii. 3.

I have been young, and now am old, yet have I not seen the righteous forsaken, nor his seed begging bread.—Psalm xxxvii. 25.

I will never leave thee, nor forsake thee.— Heb. xiii. 5.

Therefore take no thought for the morrow; for the morrow shall take thought for itself: sufficient unto the day is the evil thereof.--Mat. vi. 34.

In all their afflictions he is afflicted.—Isaiah lxiii. 9.

In that he himself hath suffered, being tempted, he is able to succour them that are tempted.—Heb. ii. 18.

### THE SHORT DURATION OF OUR TRIALS.

Weeping may endure for a night, but joy cometh in the morning-—Psalm xxx. 5.

They that sow in tears shall reap in joy.— Psalm cxxvi. 5.

Wherein ye greatly rejoice, though now for a season, if need be, ye are in heaviness, through manifold temptations.—1 Peter i. 6.

But this I say, the time is short—let those that weep be as though they wept not.—1 Cor. vii. 30.

The sufferings of this present time are not worthy to be compared with the glory to be revealed in us.—Romans viii. 18.

Our light affliction which is but for a moment,

worketh out for us a far more exceeding and eternal weight of glory.—2 Cor. iv. 17.

## ENCOURAGEMENTS TO CAST OURSELVES AND OUR BURDENS UPON THE LORD.

Call upon me in the day of trouble : I will deliver thee, and thou shalt glorify me.—Psalm L. 15.

Cast thy burden upon the Lord, and he shall sustain thee : he shall never suffer the righteous to be moved.—Psalm lv. 22.

## DIRECTIONS AND EXAMPLES HOW TO BEHAVE IN TROUBLE.

And AARON held his peace.—Lev. x. 3.

It is the Lord : let him do what seemeth him good.—1 Sam. iii. 18.

In all this JOB sinned not, nor charged GOD foolishly.—Job i. 22.

What ! shall we receive good at the hand of GOD, and not receive evil ?—Job ii. 10.

Surely it is meet to say unto GOD, I have borne chastisement, I will not offend any more. —Job xxxiv. 31.

I was dumb, I opened not my mouth, because Thou didst it.—Psalm xxxix. 9.

Father, if thou be willing, remove this cup from me : nevertheless, not my will but thine be done.—Luke xxii. 42.

My brethren, count it all joy when ye fall into divers temptations. Let patience have her perfect work.—James i. 3, 4.

### BENEFICIAL RESULT OF AFFLICTIONS.

It is good for me that I have been afflicted : before I was afflicted I went astray; but now I have kept thy word.—Psalm cxix. 67, 71.

And I will bring the third part through the fire, and will refine them as silver is refined, and will try them as gold is tried; they shall call on my name, and I will hear them : I will say it is my people : and they shall say, the Lord is my GOD.—Zech. xiii. 9.

We glory in tribulation also ; knowing that tribulation worketh patience ; and patience, experience ; and experience, hope; and hope maketh not ashamed, because the love of GOD is shed abroad in our hearts, by the Holy Ghost which is given to us.—Rom. v. 3—5.

### END OF ALL OUR AFFLICTIONS.

These are they which came out of great tribulation, and have washed their robes, and made them white in the blood of the Lamb.   Therefore are they before the throne of GOD, and serve him day and night in his temple : and he that sitteth on the throne shall dwell among them.   They shall hunger no more, neither thirst any more; neither shall the sun light on them nor any heat.   For the Lamb that is in the midst of the throne, shall feed them, and shall lead them unto living fountains of waters; and GOD shall wipe away all tears from their eyes.—Rev. vii. 14—17.

In thy presence is fullness of joy; at thy right hand are pleasures for evermore.—Psalm, xvi. 11.

Daughter of sorrow, these are the words of GOD : and they are tried words.   Millions now in glory, and myriads more on the way to it, have tried them in the dark hour of their affliction, and have found them a cordial to their fainting spirits.   " Unless thy word had sup-

ported me," they have each said, "I had per-
ished in my affliction." That word *did* support
them, and though the torrent was roaring and
rushing furiously, kept them buoyant upon its
surface, when they otherwise must have sunk.
A single text has in some instances saved the
despairing soul from destruction. Read this
selected list; what variety of representation,
what kindness and compassion of sentiment,
what tenderness of language, what beauty in
the figures, what force in the allusions, what
appropriateness in the epithets, what comprehension in the descriptions! Whose case is
omitted? Whose circumstances are untouched?
Whose sorrows are unnoticed? Remember, I
say again, this is the consolation of GOD. It
is Jehovah coming to you, and saying to you,
"Woman, why weepest thou? Is not all this
enough to comfort you? Close not thine heart
against such consolations as these. Be still,
and know that I am GOD."

## CHAPTER V.

CONFIDENCE IN GOD.

PERHAPS, as I have already supposed, in addition to the deep affliction of your being left a widow, you are left also in circumstances every way calculated to aggravate this already heavy woe. To lose your husband is of itself a cup of sorrow requiring nothing to fill it to overflowing, and embitter it with wormwood, except to have a young dependent family, and no provision for their support, or their settlement in the world. O! for that woman to be plunged into all the anxieties of business, all the fear of destitution, who never knew a care, or tasted of solicitude; for such an one, unskilled in trade, unused to labour, to have her own maintenance and that of her children to earn! To sit day after day, amidst her little fatherless circle, and witness their unconsciousness of their loss; to hear them ask why she weeps; to have her heart lacerated by questions about their father; to sit in silent solitary grief when their voices are all hushed at night, except that which issues from the cradle; to be followed to a sleepless pillow, and be kept waking through the live-long night, by recollections of departed joys, and *fears of future want!* ! Ah my afflicted friend, I pity you. May GOD support and comfort you.

Permit me to whisper in your ear, and direct to your troubled spirit, the passage I have already quoted, "LET THY WIDOWS TRUST IN ME; *for a judge of the fatherless and the widow is God in his holy habitation.*" Do consider who it is that says this. It is the omnipotent, all-sufficient GOD. It is he who has afflicted you, who says this. He authorises, he invites, he enjoins your confidence. But what do I mean by confidence? An expectation that he will provide for you: an expectation, which if it does not bring you to strong consolation, is sufficient, at any rate, to controul the violence of your grief, to check the hopelessness of your sorrows, and save you from despair: an expectation which shall prevent all your energies from being paralysed, and keep you from sitting down amidst your little helpless family, and abandoning all for lost: an expectation which leads you to say, " I do not see *how* or *whence* help is to come, but I believe it *will* come.    I am utterly at a loss to conceive how I shall be able to work my way, or provide for these fatherless children, but GOD has encouraged me to confide in him, and he is omnipotent.    I know not whence to look for friends, but the hearts of all men are in his hands, and he can turn some towards me in acts of kindness."    *This* is confidence; this is trust in GOD.    Is it necessary for me here to mention the grounds of trust ?    They are at hand in great number and force.

1. Dwell upon the innumerable exhortations to this duty, as appertaining to all states of sorrow and difficulty, which are to be found in the Word of GOD.    Scarcely one word occurs more frequently in the Old Testament than the word, " TRUST ;" nor one in the New, more frequently than " FAITH."    They stand intimately related; for indeed, if not identical in

meaning, they are nearly so. Trust in the GOD of providence means faith in him; and faith in CHRIST, means trust in him. How sweetly does one sacred writer after another catch up the word "TRUST," and roll it in innumerable echoes along the whole line of revelation. How repeatedly does the sound come from the lips of GOD himself "TRUST" in me. How often do we hear the troubled and destitute saint reply, "In thee do I put my trust." How often do the inspired penmen, after disclosing the glories of the divine character, and the infinite attributes of Jehovah, finish their description by such an admonition as this, "Put your trust in the Lord." Dwell on the power of GOD, and cannot he sustain you and your children? In casting yourselves on his boundless sufficiency, his infinite and inexhaustible resources, you do not obtrude or presume upon him; he invites, yea, commands your confidence. You do not lay down your burden on his arm unauthorised; he stretches out his arm and says, "Roll thy burden here, and I will sustain it. He asks, he promises to take

care of you.   Trust him then.   But you have
nothing, you think, but his bare promise.   Not
a friend to whom you can look; not an index
to point out in what way even *his* assistance is
to come.   Then you have the more need, and
I was almost going to add, more warrant to
trust him.   Then is the time for faith in GOD's
word, when you have nothing to look for from
man : then is the time to trust in the promise,
when you have nothing else *but the promise* to
trust to.   It is not possible to conceive of one
act of the human mind that more honours GOD,
or more pleases him, than that simple trust
which is exercised in the absence of every thing
else, as a ground of confidence, but the word of
GOD.   A widow, with a little circle of dependent
children, with no present provision, and no assured prospect of provision, who yet exercises
confidence in GOD, and believes she shall in
some way or other be taken care of, is in a state
of mind, certainly, as acceptable to GOD, as any
in which a human being can be found, and perhaps even more so.

   2. Meditate much upon the special promises

H

and gracious intimations which are made to
your own particular and afflictive case.   Go
over the passages which I have already quoted :
turn back to them again : read them repeatedly,
till you are enabled to feel their full force.
*They are God's own words to widows :* the language of the divine and infinite Comforter, to
the most afflicted class in all the school of sorrow; and ought they not to be received as such,
with all the faith and trust that are due to an
infallible being ?   Can. *he* have invited the
widow's saddened heart to words of consolation,
only to mock its sadness ?   Can he have attracted her confidence by language specially
addressed to her, only to leave her forsaken
and abandoned ?   This would not be *human*
mercy, much less *divine*.   Difficult, then, as it
may be, and must be, amidst broken cisterns,
failing springs, exhausted resources, and with
no prospect, or even indication, big as a man's
hand of the coming blessing on the distant
horizon, to trust in GOD, endeavour, dejected
woman, to do so.   Like Hagar in the wilderness, you may be near the deliverer, when you

know it not. An invisible comforter is near, and the provider may be coming, though unseen. Trust, O trust, and be not afraid. Endeavour to hush thy fears to rest, under the music and the charm of that one word, "Trust in the Lord, so shalt thou dwell in the land, and verily thou shalt be fed."

3. Another encouragement to trust, is the testimony of those who have observed the ways of Providence, and the care which it has exercised over widows. It has grown into a kind of current adage, "That whomsoever may seem to be overlooked by Providence, GOD takes especial care of widows and orphans." Who has not heard this expression, and who has not seen its verification in instances that have come under his own observation? Who could not mention the names of some whom he has seen extraordinarily provided for in their necessitous and seemingly helpless, hopeless widowhood? It has so often been my lot to see this gracious interposition of Providence, that I scarcely ever despond over the case of a widow; and the more necessitous and hopeless, so far as

human succour is concerned, the more confident do I feel of divine interference. Thus
true it is, that he who removes the arm of
flesh that sustained the wife, lends his own
arm of spirit and power to sustain the widow.
" Your maker is your husband," says the prophet ; an expression which represents Jehovah
as taking under his care all the widows in
existence.

4. Perhaps your own experience may come
in advantageously to encourage your confidence. You have been supported hitherto.
You sustained the shock of separation, which,
at one time, when anticipated, you thought
must crush your frame. You have perhaps
got through the first difficulties of your afflicted
condition : you have not been suffered to sink
hitherto. Remember GOD is the same yesterday,
to-day, and for ever. He neither grows tired
of helping, nor unwilling to help. He that has
carrried you through the first season of your
widowhood, can with equal ease, sustain you
through any succeeding one.

5. Direct your attention to the language of

Christ. " Behold the fowls of the air : for they sow not, neither do they reap, nor gather into barns ; yet your heavenly Father feedeth them. Are ye not much better than they ?— Matt. vi. 26. And this is but a repetition of a similar sentiment in Psalm cxlvii. 9. : " He giveth to the beast his food, and to the young ravens which cry." Does he take care of ravens, and sparrows, and will he not take care of *you?* Will he feed his birds, and starve his babes ? Think of the millions of millions of the animal world, that rise every morning dependent for their sustenance upon the omnipresent and all-sufficient Feeder of his creatures ; yet how few of them ever perish for want ! This consideration may not, perhaps, have struck you before, but it is one which our Lord suggested for the comfort of his disciples, and one, therefore, which with great propriety and force, may be submitted to you.

6. Consider how all creatures, rational and irrational, are under the direction and controul of God. " He has prepared his throne in the heavens, and his kingdom ruleth over all."

All orders of beings, from the highest seraph in glory, down to the meanest reptile that crawls in the dust, are his servants, and can be made to do his will, execute his plans, and fulfil the purposes of his benevolence towards his people. All hearts are at his disposal, and he can make even the covetous liberal, the hard-hearted sympathetic, and the hostile friendly. In a thousand instances he has made men act contrary to their nature, and brought as it were the waters of mercy out of the rocky heart, to refresh the weary and faint. Help has often come from quarters, whence it was to be least expected : and instruments have been employed which, to the eye of reason, were of all the most unlikely.

The following fact, extracted from an American religious newspaper, is an illustration of this.

" It was a cold and bleak evening, in a most severe winter. The snow, driven by the furious north wind, was piled into broad and deep banks along our streets. Few dared or were willing to venture abroad. It was a night which the poor will not soon forget.

"In a most miserable and shattered tenement, somewhat remote from any other habitation, there then resided an aged widow, all alone, *and yet not alone.* During the weary day, in her excessive weakness, she had been unable to step beyond her door stone, or to communicate her wants to any friend. Her last morsel of bread had been long since consumed, and none heeded her destitution. She sat at evening by her small fire, half famished with hunger,—from exhaustion unable to sleep—preparing to meet the dreadful fate from which she knew not how she should be spared. She had prayed that morning, in full faith, ' Give me this day my daily bread,' but the shadows of evening had descended upon her, and her faithful prayer had not been answered. While such thoughts were passing through her weary mind, she heard the door suddenly open, and as suddenly shut again, and found deposited in her entry, by an unknown hand, a basket crowded with all those articles of comfortable food, which had all the sweetness of manna to her. What were her feelings on that night, GOD

only knows ! but they were such as arise up to
Him—the great deliverer and provider—from
ten thousand hearts every day. Many days
elapsed before the widow learnt through what
messenger GOD had sent to her that timely aid.
It was at the impulse of a little child, who on
that dismal night, seated at the cheerful fireside
of her home, was led to express the generous
wish, that that poor widow, whom she had
sometimes visited, could have some of her
numerous comforts and good cheer. The
parents followed out the benevolent sugges-
tion : and a servant was soon despatched to
her mean abode with a plentiful supply.

"What a beautiful glimpse of the chain of
causes, all fastened at the throne of GOD ! An
angel, with noiseless wing, came down and
stirred tbe peaceful breast of a pure-hearted
child, and with no pomp or circumstance of
the outward miracle, the widow's prayer was
answered."

Of course when I recommend confidence in
GOD, it is implied that all suitable exertions be
made to obtain the means of support. If you

allow grief, despondency, and indolence to paralyse your efforts, you have no encouragement to trust in GOD. His grace is to be exercised in connexion with the employment of all those energies which yet remain : and every widow, instead of sitting down to indulge in hopeless sorrow, should, in humble dependence on divine grace, immediately apply herself in such way as her talents and her circumstances allow, to some occupation, for the support of herself and her children.

## CHAPTER VI.

### BENEFITS OF AFFLICTION.

It may not be amiss to introduce here a few of the benefits, which afflictions in general are intended and calculated to produce.  God does not afflict willingly, nor grieve the children of men.  He takes no delight in seeing our tears, or hearing our groans; but he does take delight in doing us good, making us holy, conforming us to his own image, and fitting us to dwell in his own presence.  He treats us as the sculptor does the marble under his hand, which from a rough unsightly mass he intends to carve into a splendid statue, a glorious work of art.  Every application of the chisel, every blow of the mallet, is to strike off some bit of the stone, which must be removed to bring out the figure in perfection, which he designs to form.  In our case how much is necessary to be struck off from our corrupt nature, and from what appertains to us, before we can be brought into that form and beauty which it is the intention of the divine artificer we should bear, especially as it is his plan to mould us into his own image. How much of pride and vanity; of carnality and worldly-mindedness; of self-sufficiency and independence; of creature-love and earthly dependence; must be displaced by one blow of the mallet, and one application of the chisel after another, before the beauties of holiness, humility, meekness, and heavenly mindedness; and all the graceful proportions and features of the divine nature can be exhibited.

Various authors have represented the benefits derived from affliction. *How does it quicken devotion.* Our prayers are too often only *said* in prosperity, now they are *prayed;* then they do but drop, now they are poured out, and flow like a stream, or rise like a cloud of incense, in almost uninterrupted exercise, till the thoughts and feelings seem to follow without intermission in one continued prayer. Ah! how many can look back to the place of affliction, and say,

"There it was my soul poured out many prayers to the Lord. I had grown negligent of the duty, and careless in its performance; but then I prayed indeed: then I had communion with GOD; then I sought the Lord, and he heard me and delivered me from all my fears." Nearness to GOD is the happiness of the renewed soul. Affliction is but one of GOD's servants to bring us into his presence, and the enjoyment of this privilege. GOD delights to hear from us often, as the kind parent loves to hear from his child when at a distance from home. Affliction comes and knocks at the door, enters into our habitation, asks us if we have not forgotten our father, and expresses a willingness to conduct us to him. Many have found, in trial, the lost spirit of prayer, and have experienced in that one benefit, more than a compensation for all they have suffered. Many a woman has been recalled, as a widow, to the closet of devotion, which as a wife, she had forsaken.

Affliction *discloses, mortifies, and prevents sin.* It is a season of remembrance. The sin of JOSEPH's brethren was forgotten till they were in prison; then it came to their recollection, and they exclaimed, " We are verily guilty concerning our brother." The poor widow of Zarephath, when her child lay dead in the house, thus addressed the prophet, "What have I to do with thee, O thou man of GOD? Art thou come unto me to call my sin to remembrance, and to slay my son?"—1 Kings xvii. 18. Perhaps at that moment, the guilt of all her past life, for which she had not sufficiently humbled herself before GOD, came before her perturbed mind. Sin appears but small, and presses but lightly on the conscience in the days of prosperity, but its awful form seems terrific in the night season of trial. Our sorrows look then as the shadows of sins, and address us as with a kind of spectral voice. We go back through our lives; we follow ourselves through every scene; we look at our conduct with an inquisitive and jealous eye; we examine our motives, and weigh our spirits; and oh what humbling disclosures are the result! Many have gained more self-knowledge by a month's learning in the school of sorrow, than by all their previous life. As it discloses sin, so it mortifies it. As wise and salutary discipline weakens evil habits and strengthens the moral virtues; as the frosts of winter kill, in fallow ground, the noxious insects, and the rank and poisonous weeds; as the knife prunes the tree of its dead and super-fluous branches; and as the fire purifies the precious metals, so that they lose nothing by its action, but their dross; so trials purge the soul of its corruptions, by weakening the love of sin, giving an experimental proof of its ma-lignity, awakening strenuous efforts to resist its influence, and teaching the necessity of renewed acts of faith on the atoning blood of the Saviour, and dependence on the power and grace of the Holy Spirit. "Every branch in me that beareth fruit, he pruneth it that it may bear more fruit." —John xv. 2. "By this, therefore, shall the iniquity of JACOB be purged; and this is all the fruit to take away his sin."

When Mr. CECIL was walking in the Botan-tanical Gardens of Oxford, his attention was arrested by a fine pomegranate tree, cut almost through the stem near the root. On asking the gardener the reason of this, " Sir," said he, " this tree used to shoot so strong, that it bore nothing but leaves. I was therefore obliged to cut it in this manner; and when it was almost cut through, then it began to bear plenty of fruit." The reply afforded this inquisitive student a general practical lesson, which was of considerable use to him in after life, when severely exercised by personal and domestic afflictions. Alas! in many cases, it is not enough that the useless branches of the tree be lopped off, but the stock itself must be cut— and cut nearly through,—before it can become extensively fruitful. And sometimes the finer the tree, and the more luxuriant its growth, the deeper must be the incision."*

Nor is affliction without its benefit in *preventing* sin. We never know how near we are to danger. We are like blind men wandering near the edge of a precipice, the mouth of a

* "Sympathy," p. 154, by the Rev. JOHN BRUCE, Minister of the Necropolis, Liverpool. This is a tender and inestimable volume for the afflicted in general, and especially for those who have suffered the loss of friends.

well, or the margin of a deep pit; and then GOD
by a severe wrench, it may be, and a violent
jerk that puts us to some pain, and gives us a
severe shock, plucks us from the ruin that we
saw not.   Oh what hair-breadth escapes from
destruction, effected perhaps by some distressing visitation, shall we in eternity be made to
understand, we experienced on earth.   We
now often stand amazed at some sore trial; we
cannot conjecture why it was sent; we see no
purpose it was to serve, no end it was to accomplish,—but there was an omniscient eye that
saw what we did not, and could not see, and he
sent forth this event to pluck our feet from the
net which had been spread for them.   How we
shall adore GOD in heaven for these preventing
mercies, that came in the form of some dark
and inexplicable event, which filled us at the time
with lamentation and woe!   Oh woman, even
thy husband's grave, was to prevent perhaps a
calamity still deeper and heavier than his death.

Affliction *tends* to *exercise, improve and
quicken our graces.*   In the present state these
are all imperfect, and our conformity to the

divine purity is only like the resemblance of
the sun in a watery cloud, our imperfections
envelope and obscure our excellencies; wherefore
GOD sends the stormy wind of his providential
and painful visitations, to sweep away the clouds
and cause the hidden luminary to shine forth.
How is *faith* tried, revealed and strengthened
by tribulation! ABRAHAM had not known the
strength of *his* faith, had he not been called to
sacrifice ISAAC; nor PETER his, had he not
been called by CHRIST to tread the waves. How
many have gone with a weak and faltering
belief to the river-side, and yet when there, have
had their confidence in GOD so strengthened,
that they plunged into the flood, and have
emerged, wondering at the grace which carried
them in safety through. *Resignation* has kept
pace with their call for it. There are some
graces, which, like the stars, can be seen only
in the dark, and this is one of them. As they
came to the trial, these afflicted ones saw that
their only hope was in submission, and they
sent one piercing cry to heaven, "Lord, save or
I perish. Help me to bow down with unre-

I

sisting acquiescence." It was given them; and they kissed the rod, exclaiming, " Even so, Father, for so it seemeth good in thy sight." Their *trust* and *confidence* have equalled their faith and submission. At one time they trembled at the shaking of a leaf; to their surprise they now find they can brave storms, or face lions : then it did not seem as if they could trust GOD for any thing, now they can confide every thing to him. They have been taught lessons of affiance, which in seasons of unmolested ease, seemed as much beyond their comprehension as their attainment. " Tribulation worketh patience," and if it does not accomplish this in perfection, it produces it in large measures. Oh what a blessing is patience. It is beautifully said by Bishop HOPKINS, "If GOD confirms and augments thy patience under sufferings, sufferings are mercies ; afflictions are favours. He blesseth thee by chastisements, and crowneth thee with glory, even while he seems to crown thee with thorns. A perfect patience stoops to the heaviest burdens, and carries them as long as GOD shall please, without murmuring and repining; and if that be to the grave, it knows that what is now a load, shall then be found to be a treasure.   A christian doth but carry his own wealth, his crown, and his sceptre; which though here they be burdensome, shall hereafter be eternally glorious."

The following is an extract from a letter of OBERLIN to a lady who had suffered many bereavements.

"I have before me two stones, which are in imitation of precious stones.   They are both perfectly alike in colour, they are both of the same water,—clear, pure, and clean : yet there is a marked difference between them, as to their lustre and brilliancy.   One has a dazzling brightness, while the other is dull, so that the eye passes over it, and derives no pleasure from the sight.   What can the reason of this difference be ?   It is this; the one is cut but in few facets; the other has ten times as many.   These facets are produced by a very violent operation.   It is requisite to cut, to smooth, and polish.   Had these stones been endued with life, so as to have been capable of feeling what they underwent, the one which has received eighty facets would have thought itself very unhappy, and would have envied the fate of the other, which, having received but eight, has undergone but a tenth part of its sufferings. Nevertheless, the operations being over, it is done for ever : the difference between the two stones always remains strongly marked. That which has suffered but little, is entirely eclipsed by the other, which alone is held in estimation, and attracts attention. May not this serve to explain the saying of our Saviour, whose words always bear some reference to eternity : 'Blessed are they that mourn, for they shall be comforted,'—blessed whether we contemplate them apart, or in comparison with those who have not passed through so many trials. O that we were always able to cast ourselves into his arms, like little children,—to draw near him like helpless lambs,—and ever to ask of him patience, resignation, an entire surrender to his will, faith, trust, and a heartfelt obedience to the commands which he gives to those who are willing to be his disciples ! 'The Lord God will wipe away tears from off all faces.' "

How does affliction *tend to wean us from the world, and to fix our affections on things above.* We are all too worldly.    We gravitate too much to earth.    We have not attained to that conquest of the world by faith, which is our duty to seek, and would be our privilege to obtain.    Our feet stick in the mire, and we do not soar aloft on the wings of faith and hope into the regions above us, as we ought.    We are as moles, when we should be as eagles: mere earthly men, when we should be as the angels of GOD.    With such a revelation as we possess of the eternal world ; with such a rent as is made in the clouds of mortality by the discoveries of the New Testament ; and such a vista as is opened into the realms of immortality, how easy a thing ought it to be, to overcome the world.    With the holy mount so near, and so accessible to our faith, how is it that we grovel as we do here ?    How is it that heaven is opening to present its sights to our eyes, and its sounds to our ears, and that we will neither look at the one, nor listen to the other ?    "A christian ought to be," says Lady POWERSCOURT, "*Not one who looks up from earth to heaven, but one who looks down from heaven to earth.*" Yet the multitude do neither. Instead of dwelling in heaven, they do not visit it : instead of abiding in it, in the state of their affections, they do not look at it. Hence the need, and the benefit too, of afflictions. They cover the earth with the shades of night, the pall of darkness, so that if there be any light at all, it must come from the firmament. How differently things look when seen from the chamber of sickness, or the grave of a friend! Honor, wealth, and pleasure, lose their charms then, and present no beauty, that we should desire them. We seem to regard the world as an impostor that has deceived us, and turn from it with disgust. The loss of a friend, and especially such a friend as a husband, does more to prove the truth of SOLOMON's description of the vanity of every thing beneath the sun, than all the sermons we have ever heard, and all the volumes we have ever read.

Such are a few of the benefits to be derived, and which by many have been derived from affliction. " Take care, christian," said the late

tever you meet with in your
et not your Father! When
thy rush by in triumph, while
n sorrow, listen and hear your
you, ' My son, had I loved
ive corrected them too. I give
ay of their own hearts; but to
I give sorrow, it is that I may
crown of glory that fadeth not

JOSEPH WILLIAMS, of Kidder-
minster, one of the best men of modern times,
does but give the testimony of all GOD's chosen
and tried people, where in his diary he says, "I
find afflictions to be good for me. I have *ever*
found them so. They are happy means in the
hands of the Holy Spirit to mortify my corruptions, to subdue my pride, my passion, my in-
ordinate love to the creature. They soften my
hard heart, bring me on my knees, exercise and
increase faith, love, humility, and self-denial.
They make me poor in spirit, and nothing in
my own eyes. Welcome the cross! Welcome
deep adversity! Welcome stripping Provi-
dences."

Humbled in the lowest deep,
   Thee I for my suffering bless ;
Think of all thy love, and weep
   For my own unfaithfulness :
I have most rebellious been,
   Thou hast laid thy hand on me,
Kindly visited my sin,
   Scourged the wanderer back to thee.

Taught obedience to my GOD
   By the things I have endured,
Meekly now I kiss the rod,
   Wounded by the rod and cured :
Good for me the grief and pain,
   Let me but thy grace adore,
Keep the pardon I regain,
   Stand in awe and sin no more.
                          CHARLES WESLEY.

# PART SECOND.

SCRIPTURE EXAMPLES OF WIDOWS.

## CHAPTER I.

### NAOMI, RUTH, AND ORPAH.

THE fullness and appropriateness of scripture are as delightful as they are wonderful. In that precious volume is to be found something suited to every character, every case, and every vicissitude of life. Promises, precepts, and prospects of every variety, present themselves to all who are desirous of being directed, sanctified, and comforted. But if any one should think there is nothing which meets the specialities of her case, it cannot be the widow. This living form of human woe is found in very diversified circumstances in the Word of GOD. And to these I now direct the attention of the reader.

The first example which I present is the little group of widows, consisting of NAOMI, and her two daughters-in-law.

The book of RUTH where this touching story

is to be found, was written probably by SAMUEL, as an introduction to the historical portion of scripture which immediately follows it; or else it may be regarded as a beautiful episode of the inspired narrative, containing the account of a family, which as it stands in the line of DAVID's ancestry, and therefore in that of the Messiah, is for this reason as important as its short annals are tender and interesting.

We are informed by the sacred writer of this book, that a famine having arisen in the land of Judea, ELIMELECH, a Jew of some note among his countrymen, fled with his wife NAOMI, and his two sons, MAHLON and CHILION, into the land of Moab, to which the scarcity had not extended.   How far he was justified in such a step, by which he left all the public ordinances of true religion, to sojourn in a land of idolaters, we cannot decide.   If, indeed, there were no other means of preserving *life*, it would be wrong to condemn him; but if it were only with a view to obtain a comfortable subsistence, more easily, cheaply, and abundantly, than he could do in Judea, he was to be censured; and some have considered the afflictions which befel him in the land of Moab, as an expression of the divine displeasure for resorting to it. Let us never for any temporal advantages give up such as are spiritual; for worldly ease and prosperity, purchased at the expence of religion, are dearly bought: and at the same time, let us be cautious how we pretend to interpret the affairs of providence, and to declare that event to be a work of divine displeasure, which is only one of the common occurrences of life.

One false step is often productive of a long train of consequences, which extend far beyond the individual by whom the error is committed, and involves others in danger, or distress; this is especially true in the case of a parent. ELI-MELECH, as we have already said, had two sons, MAHLON, and CHILION, who having arrived at manhood, and being removed from all intercourse with Jewish females, married two of the women of the idolatrous land in which they now dwelt. This being contrary to the Mosaic law, which forbad the Jews to intermarry with strangers, was unquestionably wrong. But what could their father expect, who had exposed them to the peril? Religious parents should neither form associations, nor contract friendships with gay worldly people, nor choose a residence for the sake of their society; for by doing this, they are almost sure to unite their children in marriage with the ungodly.

The family was now settled in Moab, and Judea seemed, if not forgotten, yet forsaken. Alas! how soon and how suddenly was the domestic circle in this case, as in many others, invaded and broken up, and all the gay visions of earthly bliss dissipated like the images of a dream. If the famine followed not this household across the Jordan, death did, for ELIME-LECH, who sought a portion for them, found a grave far from the sepulchre of his fathers, for himself. Who feels not for NAOMI? There she is a widow! and a stranger in a strange land, distant from the house of her GOD, the means of grace, the ministers of religion, the communion of the faithful;—and surrounded only by heathens, and their abominable idolatries! Still her sons are with her, and also their wives, who had, it seems, embraced the religion of their husbands. Here then was a little circle of relatives, and the worshippers of the true GOD around her, who endeavoured to hush the sorrows of her heart, and wipe away the tears from her eyes. But her cup of sorrow was now to be filled to the brim, for first one son followed his father to the grave, and then the other. Oh widows, think of her situation, bereft by this thrice repeated blow, of every relative by blood that was near, and left with two widowed daughters-in-law, and they of pagan origin, in a land of idols !

Observe now the conduct of this forlorn and desolate woman. Did she look round on her gloomy solitude and faint at the dreary prospect? No: she was evidently a woman of strong mind, and of stronger faith. She had not, perhaps, consented, but only submitted to the removal from the Holy Land. She felt in her extremity, that though far from the house and people of GOD, she was not far from his presence; and convinced of his all-mightiness, as well as of his all-sufficiency, she turned to his promise for comfort, and leaned upon his power for support. Recollecting her situation, she gathered up her thoughts, and these led her to Judea. Moab was now a land of none but melancholy associations, containing as it did, besides the wickedness of its inhabitants, the sepulchre of her husband, and of her two sons. We wonder not that she thought of her native country, and determined to return. One only attraction made her linger. How could she quit that grave, and dwell so far from it, which contained so much that was still precious to affection, and to memory. This one feeling overcome, she prepared for her sorrowful journey homewards. She had become endeared to RUTH and ORPAH, who resolved not to quit her, and chose rather to abandon their own relatives, than the mother of their departed husbands. The three widows set forth together, a melancholy group. Thinking it right to put their sincerity to the test, NAOMI addressed them in an early stage of the journey, in language, the pathos of which will be felt by every childless widow to the end of time. ORPAH yielded to her entreaties, embraced her and returned : but no persuasions could induce RUTH, the chosen of the Lord, to separate from her, and she expressed the resolution of her piety and affection in language of exquisite simplicity, beauty, and tenderness ;— " Entreat me not to leave thee, or to return from following after thee : for whither thou goest I will go ; and where thou lodgest I will lodge ; thy people shall be my people, and thy GOD my GOD. Where thou diest I will die, and there will I be buried. The Lord do so to me, and more also, if aught but death part thee and me." Such love was not to be refused, nor such a purpose to be shaken ; and they travelled on together towards the land of Judea.

On their approach to Bethlehem, the city of NAOMI, a fine testimony was afforded to this pious Jewess, of the estimation in which she was held by her neighbours and friends, for the whole city went forth to meet her, and welcome her back. The very language of their congratulation, however gratifying to her heart, as it was in one respect, pierced it as with a barbed arrow, by reminding her, in the very repetition

K

of her name, which signifies happy, of the altered circumstances in which she returned to them. "Is this NAOMI?" they exclaimed, "Is this she whom we knew so rich, so prosperous, so happy, as the wife of ELIMELECH? How changed, how broken, how desolate! Thy widow's weeds tell us what is become of thy husband : but where are thy two sons, and who is this younger widow that accompanies thee?" "Alas, alas," she replies, "it is NAOMI's self, but not now answering to her name : Jehovah in his righteous judgments, has deprived me of every thing that entitled me to the blissful designation that once belonged to me, as a joyful wife, and happy mother; call me MARAH, a name more befitting me as a poor childless widow." Amidst all, she acknowledged the hand of GOD in her bereavements, and while she gave utterance to her sorrows, did not darken the tale with the language of complaint. Four times, in the compass of her short reply, did she trace up her losses to the divine hand. "The Lord hath afflicted me," was her declaration. How much is included in that expression!

NAOMI gave not herself up to the indulgence of indolent and consuming grief, but immediately employed her thoughts in providing for the faithful and devoted RUTH, whose stedfast attachment towards GOD and herself, had been so convincingly manifested. Her conduct in this business was not that of an artful and scheming woman, busy and dexterous in contrivances for bringing about an advantageous marriage for her daughter-in-law; but of one who was well skilled in the provisions of the code of MOSES, and who knew that if a man died without issue, the next of kin unmarried, should marry his widow, and thus raise up seed to preserve and transmit the patrimonial inheritance in a right line. All her conduct, in bringing about the union of RUTH with BOAZ, however different from the habits, and opposed to the feelings of modern times, was directed with strict regard to the Levitical arrangements.

Three different classes of widows may be instructed by this narrative.

1. Those who are called to this sorrowful condition in a strange land; and such some-

K 2

times occur : such I have known, of whose sorrows I have been the distressed and sympathising spectator. I shall not soon forget the melancholy scene I witnessed when an American lady was deprived of her husband by death in my own vicinity, and left with five small children, three thousand miles from any relative she had on earth. Her husband occupied a spacious house, and extensive grounds, of which every room, and every tree, as her eye rolled listlessly round on what had once pleased her, reminded her of her utter and gloomy solitude. Others there are who are like her, for whom I cherish a sympathy, which no language can express. Your case, as a widow, even if surrounded by all the scenes of a home in your native land, and all its friends and dear relations, is sad enough; but to be away from all these; to wear your sad costume, and pour forth your tears among those who have no tie to you, and no interest in you, but what your sorrows create, and what common humanity inclines them to yield to the stranger in distress —this *is* affliction, and is to be, a " widow in-

deed." Let me, however, remind you of topics
that have, or ought to have, power to soothe
even your lone heart. Recollect, that GOD is
every where. Like wretched HAGAR in the wilderness, you may lift your eye to heaven and say,
"Thou GOD seest me." Yes, GOD with all his
infinite attributes of power, wisdom, and love,
is with you. Between you and earthly friends
continents may lie, and oceans roll, but all
places are equally occupied by your divine friend,
and are equally near to your heavenly home.
Even though you had been alone in the midst
of an African wilderness, or an American forest,
or an Asiatic heathen city, when you were called
to surrender your husband; though you had
been called to dig his grave, and lay him there
yourself, GOD could sustain you, for he is omnipotent, and all-sufficient. Lean upon his
arm; yea, trust him, though it seem in your
case to be a kind of experiment, a sort of proof
to test him, and try under how weighty a load
of care and grief he can support you. If it be
a kind of uttermost, that you are inviting him
to, he will accept, with wondrous condescension,

the invitation, and come in the plenitude of his power and grace to your help. Only believe that GOD can and will sustain you, and you *will be* sustained. The power of GOD is not weakened by your distance from the scenes of your nativity, the circle of your friends, or the comforts of your home.

2. In the conduct and character of ORPAH we find a type of those young widows who having been brought to a profession of religion during the life of a pious husband, relapse at his death into their former worldly-mindedness, and indifference to spiritual subjects. This, perhaps, is not an uncommon case. A female marries a pious man, and through his example and persuasions her mind is impressed with the great concern of salvation, and she becomes a professor of religion; renounces the world; conforms to the orders and observances of domestic worship; accompanies her husband to the house of GOD and the sacramental table; and seems in earnest about eternal salvation. In the course of Providence, her husband and spiritual guide is removed by death. During the first months

of her widowhood, while her grief is fresh and
deep, she still keeps up an attendance on all
her religious duties, and repairs to them as
almost her only comfort. But as the pungency
of sorrow abates, she becomes less and less dependent on religion for her comfort. The world
smiles on her, and she begins to return its
smiles. She insensibly loses her interest in
religion, and feels a reviving love to occupations and amusements, which during the life of
her husband, she had seemed to abjure; till at
length, her heart, after a little hesitation, goes
back to its own country, and its idols. This is
a melancholy occurrence, where the loss of the
husband is followed with the loss of the soul,
and she parts from him in the dark valley of
the shadow of death never again to meet him;
no not in heaven. He left her with the hope
of meeting her at the right hand of the judge,
and impressed his last kiss upon her cheek in
the pleasing anticipation of embracing her as a
glorified spirit in the world of glory; but she
will not be there, for she has forsaken GOD,
and returned to the world. What bitter emo-

tions will the remembrance of his holy love, and faithful care of her spiritual interest furnish in that dark world, to which her spirit will be consigned.  O woman, once wife of the pious, go not back.  Let not the piety happily commenced amidst the joys of connubial life, be dispersed by the sorrows of your widowed state!  Let the seeds of religion sown in your soul by a husband's hand, be watered by his widow's tears, and watched by her vigilant and assiduous care.  Would you be separated from him in eternity, and by a gulph so wide and so impassable as that which divides hell from heaven?  Oh, pray, and seek, and labour, that his death may be the means of perpetuating the faith which his life commenced.  Keep up the recollection of his example, his prayers, his solicitude for your spiritual welfare.  Let his blest shade, wearing the smile of piety and look of love, and with his finger pointing you to the skies, be ever before your imagination, as your guardian spirit, ministering to your salvation.

Perhaps you have children, and never can forget with what holy anxiety he endeavoured

to train them up for GOD and heaven. His
prayers for their salvation still sound in your
ears; his tears over their interests still drop
before your eyes; his last charge, as he consigned them into your hands on his dying bed,
to bring them up in wisdom's ways, yet thrills
through your soul. Oh! and shall these consecrated pledges of your affection; these living
monuments of his dear self, these offerings made
so solemnly to GOD, be carried back by you to
the world? Will you undo all that you saw
him do with such pious labour? Will you
take from the altar of GOD, those whom he had
conducted to it, and offer them at the shrine of
Mammon?

3. But turn to RUTH, and see there a female
brought by her marriage to the knowledge and
worship of the true GOD, and still retaining in
her widowhood her devotedness to him. I
again refer you to that exquisite burst of filial
love, and genuine piety, "Entreat me not to
leave thee, or to return from following after
thee; for whither thou goest I will go, and
where thou lodgest I will lodge; thy people

shall be my people, and thy GOD my GOD."
No; *she* would not go back to her country and
to her gods, but determined to go into Judea,
and serve the GOD of CHILION, her husband:
and she did.    Happy woman, and rich was her
reward!    What can so gently sooth the sorrows
of widowhood, so mollify its wounds, so raise
its fallen hopes, and sweeten its bitter cup, as
retaining the power of that religion, which
sanctifies and strengthens the marriage bond.
True it is that when a wife has found in a husband the instrument of her conversion, and
many have found it, it seems an additional aggravation to her loss, to be thus deprived of her
earthly companion and heavenly guide; but
when she holds fast the faith that she learnt
from him, she is by this means prepared to bow
with submission to the loss, and to feel her solitude more tolerable.    How sacred and how
tender are her recollections, if she retains her
stedfastness.    Nothing but what is pleasant
comes from the past into her mind.    No re-
morse of conscience smites her, as it must do
the widow who departs from the religion she

had professed in her marriage state. She never in her dreams, or in her waking hours sees her husband's frowning image looking with reproachful eye upon her. Maintaining with unbroken consistency her profession, she is soothed and comforted still, by all the holy assiduities of those of her pious friends whom his religion brought around her, and whom her own, now retains. Her heart is dead to the world, and no distance of time from his decease seems to to revive it. In communion with GOD, that GOD to whom he led her, and to whom they so frequently approached together, she finds her consolation. The seasons of their joint devotion still please and edify in recollection. The books they read together are re-perused—the place which he occupied in the sanctuary, and in the scene of domestic piety, still present him to her memory, and stimulate her devotion— the spot where they kneeled and poured out together their cares and joys in prayer and thanksgiving to GOD, rekindles from time to time the flame of piety in her soul.

Then her children, if she has any, are still

the objects of her solicitude and care. She
feels a sweet and sacred obligation upon her
conscience, to carry on that system of education
which she commenced under the direction and
with the help of her most dear husband.

She knows it to be at once her duty and her
privilege to train up for GOD, those whom she
had so often heard him commend with such
earnestness to their heavenly father.  Often as
she talks of their sainted parent till her tears
and sobs almost choke her utterance, she reminds them that if they follow his faith and
patience, they shall soon all meet in the presence of CHRIST to part no more.

Widow of the departed christian, forsake not
then the GOD of your husband, and your own
GOD too : follow him in his piety, and follow
him to glory, and let it be the solace of your
widowhood to remember, that

> The saints on earth and all the dead,
>   But one communion make ;
> All join in CHRIST their living head,
>   And of his grace partake.

And in order to cleave to your husband's GOD, cleave to his pious relatives. Imitate RUTH in this. It may be that like her, you have been called out of a circle in which true piety had neither place nor countenance. Your own relatives are of the earth, earthly, and holding lax views and sentiments with regard to religion, they are likely, if much associated with, to divert your thoughts, and turn the current of your affections away from things unseen and eternal, to things seen and temporal. They will, perhaps, wish to recover you back to your former indifference to these important matters, and propose means to recreate your spirits very alien from all your present convictions and tastes. It will be their especial effort, probably, to draw you out of the circle of your husband's religious friends, and bring you back to the gay circle you have left. Such efforts must be judiciously and kindly, but, at the same time, firmly resisted. Without alienating yourself from your own worldly friends, you must not allow yourself to be separated from his pious ones. In their society you will find, not only the most precious and sacred consolations, but the most likely means to establish you in the faith and hope of the gospel, and to perpetuate your enjoyment of its rich privileges.

This is important on account of your children also. You are desirous of bringing them up in the fear of GOD, and the love of CHRIST, according to the plan and design of their departed father : and to accomplish this, it is necessary to keep them as much as possible from such associations as would defeat your hopes, and to place them in the way of others, whose example and influence would conduce to their accomplishment. Character is formed in a great measure by imitation, and if we place the young and susceptible mind in the way of such examples as are altogether worldly, even though they may not be vicious, we are exposing them to great hazard, and are putting in jeopardy their eternal salvation.

# CHAPTER II.

---

THE WIDOW OF ZAREPHATH.—1 Kings, xvii.

---

*An example of trust and kindness to such*
*widows as are poor.*

---

The prophet ELIJAH, after having been miraculously fed during a long famine, by ravens at the brook Cherith, found it necessary to quit his retreat in consequence of the failure of the stream which had hitherto supplied him with water. There is a mysterious sovereignty running through all the ways of GOD, extending also to his miraculous operations. He works no more wonders, and gives no more signs, than the exigency of the case needs. He that sent flesh by a bird of prey, could have caused the brook still to resist the exhausting power of the drought, or have brought water out of the stones which lay in its dry bed : but he did not see fit to do so. When the brook fails, however, GOD has a Zarephath for his servant; and a widow, instead of ravens, shall now feed him; for all creatures are equally GOD's servants, and he is never at a loss for instruments either of power to destroy his enemies, or of love to succour and help his friends : what he does not find he can make, and here, therefore, is a firm ground of our confidence in him : " They that know his name will put their trust in him." " Arise," said GOD to the prophet, " get thee to Zarephath, which belongeth to Zidon, and dwell there : behold, I have commanded a widow woman to sustain thee there." Every thing in the injunction must have been confounding to reason. " What ! go to Zarephath ! a city out of the boundaries of the land of promise ! the native country of JEZEBEL, my bitterest foe ! Go to such a distance in a time of famine ! What am I to do, and how am I to be fed on my long and toilsome journey ? And when I shall have arrived there, am I to be dependent on a woman, and she a widow ?" Did ELIJAH reason, and question, and cavil thus ?

Nothing of the sort, for what is difficult to reason, is easy to faith. GOD had commanded,
and his commands imply promises. It was
enough, "Go, for GOD sends thee;" and he
went nothing doubting, nothing asking, nothing
fearing.

Arrived at the vicinity of the place about
eventide, and looking round, of course, for the
female hand that was at once to guide him to
a home, and feed him too, ELIJAH saw a
poor woman gathering a few sticks, which the
long drought had scattered in abundance. Her
occupation, as well as her appearance, proclaimed
her poverty. He saw no one else; "can that
be my benefactress?" we can fancy him asking
himself. Remembering, however, the ravens
who had been his purveyors for a whole year,
he knew that help could come by the hand of
even that feeble instrument. An impression,
such as those who had been accustomed to receive revelations from GOD well understood, assured him that his deliverer was before him.
" Fetch me," said he, " a little water in a vessel
that I may drink." Such a request was asking

L

for more than gold.    Yet awed by the prophet's appearance, and influenced by the prophet's GOD, she set out immediately in quest of the precious liquid, but was stopped to hear another request : " Bring me a morsel of bread in thy hand."    This second request drew from the poor woman one of the most affecting statements that even poverty's self ever made : " As the Lord thy GOD liveth, I have not a cake, but a handful of meal in a barrel, and a little oil in a cruse, and behold I am gathering two sticks that I may go in and dress for me and my son, that we may eat it and die."    Alas ! poor mother, thy condition is sad indeed, thou art, in thine own apprehension, about to make thy last meal, with thy fatherless child, and then with him to yield yourselves to death.    It was time for the prophet to visit this widow, to whom he was evidently sent, more on her account than his own.    How little could she have imagined when she uttered that sorrowful confession of destitution, that help was at hand, and a rich supply at her very door.    How opportunely does GOD provide succours for our distresses.    It is his

glory to begin to help, when hope seems to
end, and to send assistance in his own way,
when ours all fail, that our relief may be so
much the more welcome and precious, by how
much the less it is expected, and thus be to his
own praise, as much as it is for our comfort.
ELIJAH full of prophetic impulse, as well as
urged by hunger, said to her, " Fear not; go,
and do as thou hast said; but make me thereof
a little cake first, and bring it unto me, and afterwards make for thee and for thy son : for thus
saith the Lord GOD of Israel, The barrel of
meal shall not waste, neither shall the cruse of
oil fail, until the day that the Lord sendeth rain
upon the earth." What answer to this would
he have received from many, yea, from all who
were not as full of faith as this poor widow?
She might have said, " Charity begins at home.
My child has claims upon me, and I have a
claim upon and for myself, which it is impossible to forego or forget for any other;
and I am surprised at a request which would
take the last morsel from us both to feed a
stranger." And I do not hesitate to say, that

L 2

her compliance with the injunction, can be justified only on the ground of her faith in the
promise. That she *did* believe the promise is
evident, and equally so, that this faith was the
gift of GOD to her soul. This *was* faith, and of
no ordinary strength; it made her willing "to
spend upon one she had never seen before a
part of the little she had, in hope of more; to
part with the means of present support, which
she saw, in confidence of future supplies, which
she could not see; and thus oppose her senses
and her reason to exercise her belief in GOD's
word."\* She went and did according to the
saying of ELIJAH. And now, we ask, was she
deceived by the failure, or rewarded by the ful-
filment, of the promise? When did one word
that GOD has spoken fall to the ground? Thus
stands the record: "She and her son did eat
many days. And the barrel of meal wasted
not, neither did the cruse of oil fail, *according
to the word of the Lord,* which he spake by
ELIJAH."

---

\* See the beautiful Contemplations of Bishop HALL.

"Behold then," says the author of ELIJAH the Tishbite, "this man of GOD cheerfully sitting down in her solitary cottage. Surely 'the voice of rejoicing and salvation is in the tabernacles of the righteous;' for 'the right hand of the Lord,' on their behalf, 'doeth valiantly,'—Psalm cxviii. 15. They rejoice together, not only on account of temporal blessings, but much more on account of those which are spiritual. Israel had lost ELIJAH, and a poor widow in a heathen land has found him. Thus often does it fare with a people, who, though they have been privileged with the most faithful preaching of the gospel, will not turn unto the Lord, with all their heart, and walk uprightly before him. They are cursed with a famine of the Word of GOD; the children's bread is taken from *them,* and imparted to others whom they account no better than dogs, who however 'will receive it,' and are languishing for it. Indeed our Lord himself thus applies this part of sacred history to the case of the people of Nazareth, who refused to receive his ministry: 'I tell you of a truth, many widows were in Israel in the

days of ELIAS, when the heaven was shut up
three years and six months, when great famine
was throughout all the land; but unto none of
them was ELIAS sent, save unto Sarepta, a
city of Sidon, unto a woman that was a widow.'
—Luke iv. 25, 26. Here then the prophet
dwells quite happy under the widow's roof. All
distress has disappeared. The meal is not diminished in the barrel, nor fails the oil in the
cruse, according to the word of the Lord, which
he spake by ELIJAH. Neither does their spiritual sustenance fail. Well might this poor
widow rejoice in the privilege of sitting daily at
the feet of this man of GOD, for instruction in
divine things! Can we doubt for a moment
that the prophet most gladly opened his mouth
in divine wisdom, to impart it to the soul of
this simple believing sister? Can we doubt
that they prayed together, that they read together out of Moses and the prophets, that
they conversed together of the day of CHRIST,
which ABRAHAM saw with gladness? And
would they not, think you, occasionally raise a
spiritual song to the honour of their Lord and

Saviour? How swiftly and how pleasantly must the hours have passed with them; and well might the angels of God have rejoiced, as no doubt they did, over this little church in the wilderness! Behold here then, my brethren, the bright egress and happy termination of a path, which commenced in such thick darkness! *Only let all the children of God implicitly follow his guidance, and he will assuredly couduct them to a glorious end.*"

The trials of this poor widow, however, consisted not of her poverty alone. The child miraculously snatched from the jaws of famine was still mortal, as the event proved, for he sickened and died. In her behaviour under this new trial, we see that her faith, as a believer, was sadly mixed with her infirmity as a woman; and that it did not shine with the same lustre in this new trial, as it did in the former one. What poor changeable creatures we are, and how insufficient is past grace for present duties and afflictions. Perhaps, we are sometimes as apt to presume upon past experience, as we are, at other seasons, to forget it.

"What have I to do with thee thou man of GOD? Art thou come to call my sin to remembrance, and to slay my son?" This was the language of ignorance and passion, which we should hardly have expected from one who had seen the miracle of the barrel of meal, and cruse of oil; and shows how sorrow is apt to becloud the judgment and to exasperate the feelings; and at the same time, how affliction is apt to revive the recollections of past and even pardoned sin. ELIJAH, with a touching gentleness, which instructs us how to bear with the petulant complaints of deep grief, bore with her expostulation, and restored the child to life, and to the arms of his joyful and grateful mother. Her faith and confidence, a little shaken by the trial, returned with her son's life, and she lived, with him, to praise and glorify GOD.

And now let those to whom this beautiful narrative is especially applicable, take it to themselves, and apply it their own sad and sorrowful hearts? And who are they? The widows that are left in circumstances of deep poverty, who have only a handful of meal, as

EXAMPLES. 153

it were, in the barrel, and a little oil in the cruse; and who after eating this last supply, are preparing to yield themselves to want or death. Afflicted woman, my heart bleeds for you. The provider for your own comfort and that of your children is gone; the hand of the diligent that once made you, if not rich, yet comfortable, has forgotten its cunning, and it is your bitter lot to see the little which he left you, continually consuming, without your knowing, or even being able to conjecture, from whence the empty barrel is to be replenished. It is for such as you, to remember the words of Jehovah, " And let thy widows trust in me." You have no *other* trust, and none are so much encouraged to trust in GOD, as they whose sole confidence, the Lord is. Then, above all times, is the time to look up with hope to GOD, when we have no other to look up to. What promises are upon record for your consolation. Having already laid them before you, I will only refer to a few of them. What sweet language is that in Psalm xxxiv. 1—10, and Psalm xxxvii. Turn to your bible, and read those comforting portions of Holy Scripture. Then how cheering to the believer is the prophet's assurance, " He shall dwell on high : his place of defence shall be the munitions of rocks : bread shall be given; his water shall be sure." —Isaiah xxxiii. 16. Can any thing be more encouraging than the apostle's application to the individual believer, of the promise made to JOSHUA ? So that we may boldly say, we christians, yes, every one of us individually, The Lord is my helper. Be content with such things as ye have, then, for he hath said, " I will never leave thee, nor forsake thee." The force of this passage in the original, exceeds the power of translation : it contains five negative particles within the compass of these few words, so that literally rendered it would be, " No, I will not leave thee ; no, no, I will not forsake thee." It is one of the most emphatical and beautiful examples of the force of a negative declaration, in all the scripture. GOD seems to start back with dread and abhorrence at the thought of forsaking his people. Trust him. Not that I mean to insinuate that you are authorised to expect miraculous supplies. Your garments will not be rendered undecaying like those of the Israelites in the wilderness, nor your provisions inexhaustible, like those of the widow before us; but the GOD of providence can find you means and instruments of assistance, as effectual as if the laws of nature were suspended in your behalf. All hearts are in his hands; all events are at his disposal; all contingencies are in his knowledge and under his direction. What is wanting on your part is FAITH. *Only believe,* and perhaps you are really shut up to this; you can scarcely do any thing else.

Not that I mean to discourage effort. On this subject I have dwelt in a former part of the volume: you must, in proper season and manner, exert yourself in your own support, and that of your children; but what I mean is, that when after every disposition, and fixed determination, and collected energy, to do this, you do not see through what channel, and to what object, your efforts are to be directed; you are to believe that GOD will, in ways unknown and unthought of by you, afford you his assistance. This is your faith. In ten thousand times, ten thousand instances, as we have already remarked, he has helped poor dependent widows as effectually without a miracle, as he did the woman of Zarephath by one. The barrel of meal, and cruse of oil has been replenished as truly, though not as mysteriously, as in the case before us. And why is this case recorded, but to encourage you to trust in GOD. It was a miracle it is true, and like other miracles had the high design of confirming the revelation of GOD by his prophet; but it was a miracle of supply to one in want, intended visibly to typify and illustrate GOD's ordinary providence in supplying the wants of his people, and to encourage through all ages, the exercise of pious confidence in him. Read it with this view of it; and when the last supply is exhausted, from time to time, read it again and again, to raise the hope of a future communication from him, who heareth the young ravens when they cry. You do not know when or how it will come, but believe that it *will* come. O what a GOD-honouring grace is faith ! and as this honors *Him,* so he delighteth to honour *it.* All things are possible, and all things are promised, to him that believeth. As no miracle could be wrought, in the time when these wondrous operations were common, without faith in the subject of it ; so now, in cases of providential interposition, no manifestation of GOD's power and grace is to be looked for, but in answer to faith. I would not encourage enthusiasm, but I believe that GOD saith to his dependent and destitute people, "Be it unto you according to your faith." Do not, then, look only to see the barrel of meal gradually sinking lower and lower, but look up unto GOD who can replenish it, and with much in the former to generate doubt and fear, feel also that there is as much in the latter, to encourage faith and hope.

But there is another lesson to be learnt by the conduct of the widow of Sarepta, and that is, not to let your own grief and comparative destitution, steel your hearts against the wants of others, and close your hands to their necessities. She shared with ELIJAH the last meal she was preparing for herself and her son. Grief is apt to make us selfish, and limited circumstances to produce an indisposedness to communicate. Take heed against such a state of mind as this. Exhaust not all your tears upon yourself. There are many as destitute as you are, perhaps some far more so. You are prepared by experience to sympathise with them, and will find in sympathy a relief for your own sorrows. Nothing tends more to relieve that overwhelming sense of wretchedness, with which the heart of the sufferer is sometimes oppressed, than a generous pity for a fellow weeper.

# CHAPTER III.

---

## THE WIDOW OF ONE OF THE SONS OF THE PROPHETS.

---

*Addressed to the widows of Ministers left in destitute circumstances.*

---

" Now there cried a certain woman of the wives of the sons of the prophets unto ELISHA, saying, Thy servant my husband is dead; and thou knowest that thy servant did fear the Lord: and the creditor is come to take unto him my two sons to be bondmen. And ELISHA said unto her, What shall I do for thee? tell me, what hast thou in the house? And she said, Thine handmaid hath not any thing in the house, save a pot of oil. Then he said, Go, borrow thee vessels abroad of all thy neighbours, even empty vessels; borrow not a few. And when thou art come in, thou shalt shut the door upon thee and upon thy sons, and shalt pour out into all those vessels, and thou shalt set aside that which is full. So she went from him, and shut the door upon her and upon her sons, who brought the vessels to her; and she poured out. And it came to pass, when the vessels were full, that she said unto her son, Bring me yet a vessel. And he said unto her, There is not a vessel more. And the oil stayed. Then she came and told the man of GOD. And he said, Go, sell the oil, and pay thy debt, and live thou and thy children of the rest."—2 Kings, iv. 1—7.

By the sons of the prophets we are to understand those who were collected into a kind of
colleges, where persons, called of GOD to the
prophetic office, were trained for their future
duties, under the superintendance of inspired
men.  SAMUEL, ELIJAH, ELISHA, and probably some others, were appointed to this high
and responsible station.  Among the disciples
of these great teachers were some married men.
One of these, the scripture above quoted, tells
us died, leaving a widow involved in debt contracted by her husband, and with two children to
support.  She was sued for payment, and as
the law allowed a claim for personal service, in
default of any other means of discharging the
debt, a claim which extended, according to the
interpretation of the Jews, to a man's children,
her creditors were about to seize her two sons.
Denied mercy by the claimant, she applied in
her extremity to ELISHA, with the hope probably of obtaining his interposition with the
chief creditor, or with some other persons able
to befriend her.  She reminds the prophet of
the godly character of her husband; of his own

acquaintance with him ; and of his knowledge of the truth of her testimony to his blameless conduct. From this it seems fair to conclude, that his debts had not been contracted by prodigality, luxury, or imprudence. ELISHA listened to the widow's tale of woe, and then by an impulse from GOD, relieved her wants by the performance of a miracle. Still it was a miracle that required some exertion on her part after the means of supply were provided. Upon enquiring into what articles of value or support she had left in the house, it was found that all which poverty had left her, was a small pot of oil, which, as is well known, was then used both for diet and as an unguent. This she was directed to produce, and at the same time, to go and borrow all the vessels which she could well get together in a short time, and in a small room. These having been procured, she was directed to pour the oil into them. She complied with the orders, and the oil continued to flow and to fill the vessels, till there was enough, upon its being sold, to pay her husband's debts, and save her sons from servitude.

M

Here again was an instance of faith. She knew the word of the prophet was the word of GOD, and she believed it, confidently expecting the relief which she needed. ELISHA, it is true, had not in so many words promised to grant a supply of oil, but she understood his command to borrow the vessels, in this light, and therefore collected them, both large and numerous ones. And the oil continued flowing as long as she had any empty vessels to receive it, and had her faith been greater, her supply had been raised in proportion to it. We are never straitened in GOD, in his power, or grace, but in ourselves. It is our faith that stops, or fails, and not his promise. He is able to do exceeding abundantly above all that we ask or think. "And if this pot of oil was not exhausted as long as there were vessels to receive it, shall we fear lest the 'golden oil' (of divine grace) which flows from the very root and fatness of the good olive tree, should fail, as long as there are any lamps to be supplied from it?" Zech iv. 12. How well and deservedly is faith called precious. How many has it sanctified,

comforted, and saved. Why the prophet relieved her in this way, we know not, except it
were to bring out her faith, her industry, and
her honesty, all in one view, and in beautiful
harmony. Certain it is that all these were exhibited; her faith in receiving the promise; her
industry in collecting and selling the oil; and
her honesty in paying the debts with the produce.

"Your fathers where are they, and the prophets do they live for ever?" "All flesh is as
grass, and all the glory of man as the flower
of grass. The grass withereth, and the flower
thereof falleth away; but the word of the Lord
endureth for ever. And this is the word, which
by the gospel is preached unto you."—1 Peter,
i. 24, 25. Yes, the word is immortal, but the
preacher of it is mortal. Ministers die like
other men. Life worketh in their hearers, but
death in them. They not only die *in* their
work, but often *by* it. They sink to the grave
worn out by labour, and usually leave their
widows and children ill provided with the riches
of this world. Here and there an individual

M 2

attains, by the bounty of Providence, to comparative wealth, but these are the exceptions : the general rule of ministerial circumstances is, if not poverty, an approach to it. To them it is given to say, with the great apostle of the Gentiles, "poor, yet making many rich." Blessed with talents, which, in other occupations, would be sufficient to procure competence, if not wealth, they give themselves in most cases, wholly to the things of the Lord. The consequence of this is, that with the most rigid economy, they are with difficulty able to obtain support, much less to amass property. Considering their acquirements, mental capacity, and rank in life, they are the worst paid public functionaries in existence. But they look not for their reward from men, or upon earth. They serve a master infinitely rich, and infinitely generous, and amidst much ingratitude and injustice from their flocks, they can leave their services and their reward with him. It is vain, however, to deny that it costs them many an anxious hour, when breaking down under their exertions, to contemplate the moment of their removal from this world. Not that they have any thing to fear for themselves; for them it will be better to depart and to be with CHRIST. They are going to rest from all their labours, and all their cares—but the prospect of leaving a widow and fatherless children, to the generosity of a congregation which was never over liberal while they lived, and is likely soon to forget them in affection for their successor, requires strong confidence indeed to suppress the fear, and even the groan of painful anxiety.

The dying fears, the last he will ever know, of the good man, oftentimes prove but too prophetic, as you his forlorn and desolate widow, too well know. You are indeed to be pitied. He who, in relation to you, united the husband and pastor, is removed; he whose love in your own house was your solace as a wife, and whose sermons in the house of GOD, were your comfort as a christian, is gone for ever. *You* are the centre of that grief of which the congregation are the wide circle. It is pain enough to see that pulpit occupied by another, which he once and so long filled; and to hear another

voice than his sound forth the message of life :
but other woes aggravate this already heavy
one.    They loved him and valued his ministry,
perhaps, while he lived, and it seemed as if he
had prepared for himself an imperishable monument in every heart, and would be long and
gratefully remembered by those, on whose hallowed recollections he had strong claims ; and
who, it might have been expected, would love to
demonstrate and perpetuate their gratitude, in
sympathy for his widow, and beneficence to his
children.    But *you* have proved how little reliance is to be placed upon posthumous affection.    You were prepared, or ought to have
been, to witness a transfer of that respect and
affection which had been cherished for the former pastor, to his successor ; it is right and
proper it should be so ; and you ought to rejoice and feel thankful that the church, for
which your husband laboured so hard, prayed
so fervently, and which pressed so heavily on
his spirit, in his last and suffering hours, is so
comfortably settled with one to follow in his
footsteps, and to carry on his usefulness :—but

you were *not* prepared, how could you be? to see him so soon forgotten, and to hear comparisons unkindly made, and indelicately conveyed to you, between him and his successor, and to his disparagement. You were *not* prepared, how could you be? to find his widow neglected, his children forsaken: to feel so soon that you were left, though surrounded with numerous friends, that *once* were competitors for your friendship, to mourn apart and unpitied. You were *not* prepared, to learn how much of former attention was paid you for your husband's sake, and how soon you would find this out when he was removed. Nor is this the last or the lowest step in the descending scale of your sorrows. When your husband died, the means of your support died with him, and you are now cast with your children, upon Providence for support. You expected a little more generous and practical sympathy, from a church in whose spiritual welfare your husband wore out his strength; and are bitterly disappointed that all those professions of attachment, which it was your privilege, at one time, to hear so profusely lavished on him, have ended, in results, so far as you are concerned, so miserably disproportionate.

Should all this really *be* the case with any whose sorrowful eye shall read these pages, I recommend to them the consideration, that provided their faith and trust be equal to the emergency, the less they receive from man, the more they may expect from GOD. Bear this heavy trial with meekness and a quiet spirit. Do not shew resentment; and endeavour to *feel* none. Bring no accusation and utter no complaint, much less reviling. Silent and patient submission is most likely to draw attention upon your circumstances. Many a widow in your situation, has injured her own cause by reproachful reflections upon the people of her late husband's charge. A modest but not servile appeal, laid in confidence before some of your friends, on behalf of his necessitous children, may be properly made, and ought to be attended to; and in order to engage those friends, take care that your children be well trained. It must be confessed, that in many instances, the want of interest and sympathy for the widow and children of a minister of religion, is to be traced, not so much to the want of kind feeling on the part of the people, as to her want of good sense and good temper, and their destitution of good training, and good conduct. If she be unreasonable in her expectations, and petulant and disrespectful in the event of their not being fulfilled; or if the children be rude, refractory, and unlovely through deficiency of maternal restraint; it requires much stronger generosity or affection, than is usually met with even among professing christians, to overcome so much that is repulsive, and to be kind to the living, only for the sake of the dead. Amidst the deficiencies or the scantinesses of human sympathy, look for it from a source where it never fails. God observes your situation, and beholds you as the relic of one whom he delighted to honour. You can go to *Him* with boldness and say, " Thy servant is dead who feared thee; look in pity on those whom he has left in poverty and difficulty." If such a plea prevailed with the prophet, will it not with God?

He is no debtor to you, or to your late husband; but he is a generous master to his servants, and rewards them in a way of grace, in a manner that is often surprising. If he takes care of widows and fatherless children in general, how confidently may those expect his kind interposition, who belonged to his own servants? Go then with humble boldness to the Lord Jesus, carry your children in the arms of your faith, place them in his presence, and say with all reverence and humility, but with all confidence, " Behold the children of thy departed servant." Remember that more is expected from you than from others. The widow of a minister should be an example to all widows. Col. Hutchinson, when taking leave of his wife, admonished her not to forget her standing, and to mourn as a woman of no ordinary character. How suitable is this to the widow of a teacher of religion; and how much does it become her to shew, by the manner in which she bears his death, how well she had profited by the instructions of his life. His sermons on submission to the will of God, should all appear embodied in her meek and pious resignation.

If there are sources of pain, peculiar to the
widow of a minister, there are also sources of
comfort. The memory of such a man is blessed.
You were the companion of one who wore out
life, not in amassing wealth, but in winning
souls to GOD : not in enriching himself with
filthy lucre, but in conferring upon others, imperishable wealth. Look back upon his holy
and useful career. Call to recollection his labors
for CHRIST: his trials and discouragements;
his joys and successes. Think how he served
his master, and how his master honoured him;
with what untiring zeal, amidst what self-denial,
and with what result, he pursued his holy calling.
Dwell upon his blameless character, his spotless
reputation, and the esteem in which he was held
by the churches of CHRIST. Remember how
often he prayed rather to die than be permitted
to live and sin. He was faithful unto death,
and laid down his office, only with his life.
None blush for *him,* but all weep for themselves,
before his monument. Even the tongue of
slander is silent at that hallowed spot, and dares
not utter in whisper a single insinuation. Oh

this is balm to a widow's heart. And then look at the fruits of his ministry. Some have preceded him to glory, and are his joy and crown of rejoicing in the presence of CHRIST, while others are following him on to add new gems to his diadem, and new delights to him that is to wear it. Dwell not only on what he was, and what he is, but on what *you* were to him : how you aided him in his ministry; not indeed by writing or preaching his sermons, but by sustaining that noble heart, which dictated all his labors, and by the impulses and energies of which all were sustained. Call to recollection, how he reposed in your faithful bosom the cares of office, and asked your counsels amidst its intricacies; how when he came home agitated and perplexed, you calmed the perturbations of his spirit; how when discouraged, you cheered him ; how you suggested to him subjects for his pulpit ministrations, which had occurred to you in your own meditations, and which thus became the means in his lips of saving souls from death; how you aided him in his visitations and ministrations to the sick, the poor, and dis-

tressed; and how by your earnest prayers, you
brought down upon his labours the dew of heaven; and thus, by all these means, were a help
meet for him in his high embassy to a revolted
world. These efforts, it is sadly true, are all
suspended by his death, but to have made them
is a precious remembrance. Such recollections
fall not to the lot of ordinary women, and ought
to be a balm for your wounded heart.

If you are happy amidst the people to whom
your husband ministered, remain where you
are; linger still at the pulpit in which he laboured, and at the grave where he sleeps : if
they love his memory, and are kind to you and
your children for your own sakes, as well as for
his, where can you be more happy on earth,
than in the scene of his living exertions and in
the vicinity of his tomb. Where will his precious name be so frequently and so respectfully
mentioned, and where will sympathy be so fully
felt and so tenderly expressed, as among the
people of his charge. But, then, let wisdom
and circumspection characterise your conduct.
A minister's widow has sometimes aided, not a

little, to disquiet the mind of his successor, and to trouble the circle of his friends. Excite no suspicions, awaken no jealousies, institute no comparisons. Do not wish for influence; be not the centre of a party; attempt not to guide the opinions of others; and avoid all private interference and meddling with church affairs. The importance of this, is in exact proportion to the esteem in which you are held. There are few women so weak, as to have no power to do mischief, for it is surprising and grievous to find what insignificance, when combined with restlessness, and a meddling propensity, may be a source of annoyance, and a cause of disquiet, especially in small communities. In some cases where for instance, there may not be the best understanding, nor much good feeling, between the widow and the flock; or where a part only of that flock might happen to be attached to her, and not equally attached to the new pastor and his wife; prudence and propriety combine to make it her duty, if not prevented by circumstances, to retire. It is a deep blot on the christian reputation of any minister's widow to remain in a church, only to be a neucleus of dissatisfaction and discontent, and to aid in disturbing, perhaps, dividing the society, whose peace, was one great object of her husband's life.

After all, however, it must be confessed, that where the widow and family of a minister, meet with neglect, from the congregation, in which he laboured, and some such cases do occur, both in the Church of England, and amongst the Dissenters, the fault is, in many cases, to be traced up to a want of generosity on the part of the people.

# CHAPTER IV.

---

## THE WIDOW CASTING IN HER TWO MITES INTO THE TREASURY.

---

*Illustrating the character of the poor but liberal widow.*

---

" And JESUS sat over against the treasury, and beheld how the people cast money into the treasury : and many that were rich cast in much. And there came a certain poor widow and she threw in two mites, which make a farthing. And he called unto him his disciples, and saith unto them, Verily I say unto you, that this poor widow hath cast more in, than all they which have cast into the treasury : for all they did cast in of their abundance ; but she of her want did cast in all that she had, even all her living."—Mark xii. 41—44.

THE treasury here spoken of, we should suppose, was a large chest fixed near the entrance to the temple and divided into different compartments, for receiving the offerings of the people. These were appropriated to the purpose for which the donor presented them;

some for the repairs of the building; others for the expences of public worship; and some, perhaps for the relief of the poor. The chest was well placed. Piety and liberality should be always associated. Piety should stimulate charity; charity should be the fruit of piety. On one occasion, CHRIST placed himself opposite this receptacle of benevolence, to watch the offerings of the people. The affluent passed on and deposited their wealth; for "they cast in *much*." This is so far to their credit; they who possess much, should give much. GOD expects it, yea, demands it. Among the richer worshippers came one who united in her circumstances the double affliction of poverty and widowhood. She, of course, will offer nothing. She needs to receive, rather than to impart. All she has to bestow, it may be presumed, is her good wishes. But, no; *her* hand is not empty. She drops two mites—a farthing. Perhaps the smallness of the sum excited a smile of contempt from some proud proprietor, as he followed her, and magnified, by contrast, the amount of his own contribution. But there

N

was another eye that watched the widow's offering, and another mind that drew a contrast. And CHRIST called his disciples unto him and said, "Verily I say unto you, that this poor widow hath cast more in, than all they which have cast into the treasury." Yes, *there* is the scale on which the Saviour estimates the amount of *our* contributions to the cause of religion and humanity; not abstractly by the sum given, but by the sum given in proportion to the wealth possessed. A mite from one, is vastly, incalculably more, than a pound from another. Much and little, are relative terms. That would be munificence in one, which would be niggardliness in another. No commendation had been pronounced on the gifts of the wealthy; for they had, perhaps, after all, given little compared with what they retained; but this widow's offering has immortalised her. She gave *all she had*. We do not stay to enquire about the prudence of her contribution, whether it was proper to bestow her last farthing; doubtless there were some circumstances in her case which justified the act, and with which the Saviour

was acquainted.   There were, perhaps, no needy
children, whose wants should have reminded her
that charity begins at home : perhaps it was a
thank-offering for some special mercy received;
some gracious support in one of those troubles,
which widows, and especially poor widows, only
know.   At any rate, the gift and its principle,
attracted the notice, and drew forth the eulogy
of the Saviour.   It was but a farthing, but that
farthing was as much a manifestation of her
disposition, as DAVID's almost countless amount
of gold, was of his.

Our Lord JESUS CHRIST still holds his seat
opposite the treasury of the temple, and watches
from his throne in heaven, the offerings of
those who give to the cause of religion and
humanity.   His celestial glory has diminished
nothing of his condescending regard to the beneficence of his people.   It should be our aim
in all the good we do, to approve ourselves to
his all-seeing eye, both by the purity of our
motives, and the amount of our donations
Alas what are we the better for the notice of
those perishing and impotent eyes, which can

only view the outside of our actions; or for that word of applause which vanisheth on the lips of the speaker? Thine eye, O Lord, is piercing and retributive. As to see thee, is perfect happiness, so to be seen of thee, is true contentment and glory.

It may be fairly inferred from this passage, that the Lord JESUS, while he beholds with favour the gifts of all, receives with especial acceptance the offerings of the poor widow. It is often the sorrow of such, in this age of christian missions, that they cannot share in the glorious undertaking of converting the world to CHRIST. In happier times, when the candle of the Lord shone in their tabernacle, and the light of prosperity irradiated their path, they too had something to give, and delighted to give it, to pour the blessings of salvation on this dark earth: but now they feel shut out from the feast of benevolence, and denied all fellowship in the great work of evangelising the nations; for they have nothing to give. Nothing? "Nothing," you reply, "worth my giving, or any society's receiving!" Is that the language of pride, despondency, or parsimony? Can you not, then, stoop to give a penny, after you have had the privilege of giving a pound? Do you blush to offer the copper, after the silver and gold have glittered in your hand, as you approached the treasury? O woman, cast away that feeling, and carry your two mites, and if given "with a glad heart and free," that little offering will draw upon it a more benignant smile from the Lord of all, than ever he bestowed upon your costlier gifts in the days of your prosperity. If you are ashamed to give it, he is not ashamed to receive it, nor backward to reward it. Ashamed of your little! Why it is relatively more than the hundreds of the rich. It is all self-denial, and sacrifice, and generous zeal.

"In the obscurity of retirement, amid the squalid poverty, and the revolting privations of a cottage, it has often been my lot to witness scenes of magnanimity and self-denial, as much beyond the belief, as the practice of the great; an heroism borrowing no support, either from the gaze of the many, or the admiration of the

few, yet, flourishing amidst ruins, and on the
confines of the grave; a spectacle as stupendous
in the moral world, as the falls of the Missouri,
in the natural; and like that mighty cataract,
doomed to display its grandeur, only where there
are no eyes to apprehend its magnificence."
Yes, there is an eye that looks on both, but with
more admiration on the little offering of benevolence that drops unheeded and unheard by
man, into the receptacle of mercy, than on the
river that falls with the roar of thunder into the
basin of its mighty waters. Think of aged
widows sacrificing the sugar of their tea, and
poor men giving up the small portion of their
beverage at dinner, to save a mite or two for
the missionary cause: O how little are the offerings of the rich, though the announcement
of their hundreds from the platform makes the
building to shake with applause, compared with
the penny of such self-denying friends to the
cause as these, but whose contributions find
their way in silence, to the mighty aggregate of
funds. Ashamed, my friends! Your mites
are the richest trophies of our cause; and if it

were possible to divide the results of our success, and apportion so much usefulness to each particular contribution of property, we should find, perhaps, the richest allotment assigned to the widow's farthing.

Is there a less worthy motive, that holds back your slender offering? Is there a feeling of grudging? A reasoning in this strain,— " Surely they cannot take the poor widow's penny for the cause of missions." Certainly not, unless she feels it to be one of poverty's deepest woes, to have nothing to give to *such* an object, and would esteem herself unhappy, if her little contribution were despised. Have you *nothing* then to give for widows poorer than yourself? " Poorer than myself," you exclaim, in a tone of indignant surprise, " who *can* be poorer than I am?" I answer, the Pagan woman, left forlorn and desolate, without a bible, a sabbath, or a minister, to direct her to the widow's God: and there are millions of such. *You* have the gospel, which abolishes death, and brings life and immortality to light. *You* can look beyond the grave, and see the orb of celestial day rising in majesty before the eye of christian hope, and gilding with his glorious effulgence, the dark clouds which collect over the valley of the shadow of death. *You* hear voices of joy, and sounds of life, floating like heavenly music, over the still chambers of mortality. In pity, then, to those who clasp the urn in silent despair, give a little, even of your little, to send them the gospel, which keeps *you* from sorrowing as others which have no hope. Have compassion on the widows that sit down by the grave of a husband, who has gone away in the darkness of paganism, or who still, in some parts of India, are doomed to mingle their ashes with his, in that funeral pile, the flame of which is kindled by the hand of a first-born son. Is there not, then, a widow far more wretched than yourself, for whom the scant penny of poverty, or the two mites of all but absolute destitution, should be consecrated to GOD?

# CHAPTER V.

### WIDOW OF NAIN.

*Addressed to widows who are called to lose their children also.*

" And it came to pass the day after, that he went into a city called Nain ; and many of his disciples went with him, and much people. Now when he came nigh to the gate of the city, behold there was a dead man carried out, the only son of his mother, and she was a widow : and much people of the city was with her. And when the Lord saw her, he had compassion on her, and said unto her, Weep not. And he came and touched the bier ; and they that bare him stood still. And he said, Young man, I say unto thee, arise. And he that was dead sat up, and began to speak. And he delivered him to his mother."—Luke vii. 11—15.

THE mercy of CHRIST, as it never wanted objects in this sorrowful world, so it was never wearied in relieving them. One day de healed the servant of the centurion, upon being earnestly solicited to do it, to show what efficacy there is in the prayer of faith ; the next, he restored to life the son of a widow, without being asked, to demonstrate his sovereignty in the

bestowment of his favours.   One act of beneficence seemed only to make him more ready
and more willing to perform another; in this
also he is an example to his people, who are
not to satisfy themselves with any measure of
good works.

But let us attend to the present instance of
his miraculous kindness.   As he drew near to
a small town called Nain, a funeral procession
was coming out at the gate, and was slowly
moving towards the place of sepulture, which,
with the Jews, was always without the walls of
their cities.   It was not accidental that the
Saviour came up just at that time, but was
ordered for the glory of God.   Here was a
spectacle to move a harder heart than that of
CHRIST.   The victim of death was in this instance, a young man, cut off in the flower of
his age, and on that account, a loss to society,
but a still heavier loss to that venerable form,
which, with the attire of a widow, as well as the
low moans of a bereaved mother, is following
the corpse to its last home.   It is a short, but
simply touching narrative, which the historian

gives, " Behold, there was a dead man carried out, the only son of his mother, and she was a widow." When the scripture would convey the most impressive idea of the depth of human sorrow, it uses this form of speech, " As one that is in bitterness for an only son." There it is before us, in that forlorn widow. It is afflictive to see a loving *couple* following an only child to the grave ; but then, they consider, as with tearful eyes they look upon each other, that there might have been a grief still harder to be borne, than even *this*. " Thank GOD," they exclaim, " *we* are spared to each other," and thus they find, even at the opening grave of an only child, a supporting thought in the presence of each other. But here is a case in which there is no one to share the grief, and support the fainting heart of this sorrowful woman : her husband is already in the grave, and her son, her only son, is about to be laid on the coffin of his father. At this juncture the Son of GOD drew nigh :

> His heart is made of tenderness,
> His bowels melt with love.

The widow's sorrows touched that heart: and he said to her, "Woman, weep not." Oh if she was not too much absorbed in grief to heed him, what must she have thought of such an injunction: "Who has cause to weep if it is not I. If tears are ever in season, they are now. Stranger cease to taunt me with such an exhortation, unless you can restore to my widowed arms, the child that lies sleeping there in death." She knew not who it was that spoke to her, but she shall *soon* know to her unutterable joy. As the Lord of life and death he arrests the coffin, and frees the prisoner. "Young man, I say unto thee, arise." That is the voice that shall one day burst every tomb, call up our vanished bodies, from those elements into which they are resolved, and raise them out of their beds of dust, to glory, honour, and immortality. The grave shall restore all it receives, whether that grave be in the sea, in the dry land, in the forest, the wilderness, or in the crowded cemetery. "Why should it be thought a thing incredible that GOD shall raise the dead?" It is no harder for the Almighty word, which gave being unto all things, to say, "Let them be restored," than "let them be made." The sleeping youth obeyed the mandate, rose upon the bier, cast off his grave clothes, descended, and threw himself into the arms of his astonished, enraptured, and overwhelmed mother. Blessed type of that wondrous scene just alluded to, when at the sound of the last trumpet, this mortal shall put on immortality, and this corruptible shall put on incorruption, and death shall be swallowed up in victory. I attempt not, for who could succeed in the effort, to pourtray the mother's joy, and her renewed intercourse with her lost child : all she could find composure enough to say, was "Rejoice with me, for this my son was dead, and is alive again !"

I now turn to those who are appointed to bear like sorrows, without the immediate prospect, or the hope of her relief; I mean those widows, and such there are, who have been called to part from an only child. Forlorn, indeed, is your situation—desolate your house —bereaved your heart of its last earthly hope.

Not to sympathise with you, not to concede the greatness of your calamity, would be the most cruel insensibility, such as I pray God to preserve me from.

But stop, is *all* dead? Your husband is dead, your parents are dead, your children are dead—but is not God alive—is not Christ alive—is not the bible alive? Has the tomb swallowed up all? No. Be this your exultation, "He lives and blessed be my rock, and let the God of my salvation be exalted." True, you cannot expect that the power of Christ will be exerted, at least, till the resurrection, to call your only child from the grave : but the same heart that pitied the widow of Nain, pities you. Jesus sees you as certainly, and compassionates you as tenderly as he did her, although his compassion may not be exerted in precisely the same manner.

Perhaps that only son was the last thing that stood between you and the Saviour to detain your heart from him. You had not been weaned from the world till he was taken. You still sought your happiness on earth. Your whole soul was bound up in that child. Even for God and CHRIST, you had no supreme love, while he lived : and as there was a purpose of eternal mercy to be fulfilled, by the death of that child, it pleased God to remove him. You would not come to CHRIST while that obstacle was in the way, and therefore God displaced it : now, the way to the cross is all clear. The Saviour has come to the widow, not indeed to raise her son, but to save her soul : not to say to him, "Arise young man;" but to say to you, "Arise, and be saved." If by the loss of your only son, you should gain the salvation of your immortal soul, you will find a present solace for your sorrows, and an eternal source of gratitude that they were sent.

But what are you to do without him? Let God answer that question; "*I* will never leave thee, nor forsake thee." Your child was your comforter. Be it so : but is there not a divine comforter, who frequently reserves his choicest consolations, for the most disconsolate seasons. Your son was your support. This, I admit, is trying to faith and confidence in God. A dependant widow, to lose the only child on whom she leaned for support, seems the last extremity of human destitution. It is in such extremities GOD loves to put forth his power. He often brings us into a very wilderness, to show us his own all-sufficiency. He strips us of the last comfort, and then says to us, " Now trust in me for every thing."

There are other considerations which should induce submission even to *your* melancholy lot. Heavy trials are sometimes sent to prevent heavier ones still. There are calamities, worse than death; either our own death, or the death of our nearest friends. It is better to die in honour, than to live in sin and disgrace. How many widows are there whose only sons are breaking their mother's hearts by their misconduct? Is not many a mother at this moment exclaiming thus, in her solitude, " O my child, would GOD the grave had covered thee, whilst thou wert yet in reputation, and comparative innocence! Alas! that thou shouldest have lived to disgrace thyself, and bring down thy widowed mother's grey hairs in sorrow to the grave !"

I remember to have read, or heard somewhere, the following anecdote. A widowed mother had an only son, who while yet a youth, was seized with an alarming illness. Her heart was in the greatest tumult of grief at the prospect of his removal. She sent for her minister to pray for her child's recovery. It was his preservation from death that was to be the subject of the minister's petitions, rather than the mother's submission to the will of GOD. Like a faithful pastor, he begged her to controul her excessive grief and solicitude, and resign her son to GOD's disposal: but to no avail: it seemed as if she neither could nor would give him up. Prayer was to pluck him from the borders of the grave, whether GOD were willing to spare him or not. Her son lived: the mother with ecstatic joy, received him back, as from the borders of the tomb. He grew to adult age; but it was to die in circumstances ten thousand times more afflictive to the mother's heart, than his earlier removal would have been. As he came to manhood he turned out profligate, extravagant, dishonest. His crimes be-

o

came capital; he was detected, tried, convicted, and sentenced to be hanged: and seven years from the day when that minister prayed for his life, he had to visit this wretched mother, to be with her, and comfort her, if, indeed, her heart could receive consolation, on the day of his execution. Oh! widow is there not a heavier calamity than the death, in ordinary circumstances, of an only son? I would not for a moment suggest that it is probable your son would have come to this: but it is *possible:* or if not to this, yet to something that would have embittered all your future days. Would not this distressed woman, look with envy upon others whose children had died in honour and reputation, and think their affliction not worthy of the name, compared with hers? Would she not look back with deep compunction upon her own rebellious grief and unwillingness to give up her child at the will of GOD?

Before I close this chapter, I would suggest, that as the death of an only child removes from your widowed heart, the last hope or object of a terrestrial nature, that seemed to give interest

to earth, or occupation upon it, you should look
for objects of another kind: even such as are
spiritual, heavenly, and divine. Seek, then,
not only for a richer enjoyment of personal religion, as the chief source of consolation, but
cherish a warmer zeal for its diffusion, as the
best and happiest occupation that can employ
your faculties, or your time. Now that GOD
has taken from you *your* son, adopt the cause
of *his* Son. Consecrate yourself afresh to the interests of evangelical piety. What have you now
to do on earth; what is left for you to do; what
can you find to do; but diffuse by your property,
if you possess much, and by your personal labours, if you are in health, the benefits of the
gospel, the blessings of salvation, to those who
are destitute of them? Live, now, wholly for
GOD, and the salvation of the human race.
Soften the weight of your cross, by making
known the glory of the cross of CHRIST. Instead of retiring into seclusion, to nourish woe,
to leave your sorrow to prey upon your heart,
or to let life fret itself away amidst the indolence of grief, rouse your spirit for holy action.

Let *your* loss be the gain of others, by your employing your leisure for their benefit. Freed from every tie that bound your soul to personal or relative objects, feel at liberty for doing good to others. Active benevolence is the best balm for such wounds as yours. Allow yourself no leisure for dark and melancholy thoughts to collect, or for busy memory to torment you with distressing recollections. Your departed child wants not your property; give it to God; nor your time, nor your solicitude; give them to God. In pitying the sorrows of others, you will find a sweet solace for your own. Occupy your lone heart, and hours as lonely as your heart, with schemes of mercy, and purposes of beneficence. If your affliction shall lead to such a result, you may then say of active benevolence, that it is one of—

> The best reliefs that mourners have,
> And makes their sorrows blest.

# CHAPTER VI.

## ANNA THE PROPHETESS.

### *A pattern for aged widows.*

" And there was one ANNA, a prophetess, the daughter of PHANUEL, of the tribe of Aser : she was of a great age, and had lived with an husband seven years from her virginity ; and she was a widow of about fourscore and four years, which departed not from the temple, but served GOD with fastings and prayers night and day. And she coming in that instant, gave thanks likewise unto the Lord, and spake of him to all them that looked for redemption in Jerusalem. And when they had performed all things according to the law of the Lord, they returned into Galilee, to their own city Nazareth. And the child grew, and waxed strong in spirit, filled with wisdom ; and the grace of GOD was upon him. Now his parents went to Jerusalem every year at the feast of the Passover."—Luke ii. 36—41.

THE Holy Spirit of God, while he passes over in silence the names of mighty kings and potentates, with all their civil and military achievements, their battles and their victories, writes the life, and pronounces the eulogy of a poor and pious aged widow, of whom the world

knew little and cared less, to preserve her
memory to the end of time, and to shew how
grateful to him such a kind of life is. ANNA
was one among the few who, in that dark de-
generate age, preserved the light of true piety
from being quite extinct, and who waited for
the consolation of Israel. Having lost her
husband, after a short union of seven years, she
continued a widow ever afterwards; and was
eighty-four years of age at the time of our
Lord's birth. Gifted with the spirit of pro-
phecy, she delivered the messages of GOD to
the few who were disposed to receive them, and
spake of Him that was to come, who should
bring deliverance for his people. Her abode
was in one of the dwellings which surrounded
the temple, and her sole employment devotion.
She had long been dead to the world, and the
world to her; and, with her heart in heaven,
she had neither interest nor hope upon earth.
It was her privilege, as it was of good old
SIMEON, before she closed her eyes on things
terrestrial, to see Him of whom the prophets
spake. Having uttered her gratitude that the

light had not departed from her eyes, till she had seen the Lord, she confessed him before others, and commended him to their regards. Happy saint, to see this new-born Saviour as the star of thy evening; thou hast lived to good purpose, in thus having thy existence prolonged, to welcome to our world, him who came to be its Redeemer: and now what can induce a wish to remain longer from thy Father's house? Thou mayest be willing to lay down thy tabernacle and thy widowhood, and go to that world, where thou shall flourish in the vigour of immortal youth.

And now, leaving ANNA, I turn to the aged widow, who has little to do but to wait and watch for the coming of her Lord. Mother in Israel, I address you with sentiments of reverent respect, while I call upon you to indulge the reflections, and perform the duties, appropriate to your circumstances. Your age, connected with your widowhood, renders you an object of deep interest. You have outlived, not only the husband, but the friends, of your youth. As regards those who started with you in life,

you are alone in the world; and you sometimes feel a sadness come over you, because
there are none who can talk with you of the
scenes of your childhood and youth, which are
as a tale written only in your own memory.
Spend the evening of your days, in adoring the
GOD that has kept you thus long, and in admir-
ing the varied displays of his attributes, and the
rich and seasonable communications of his
grace, which it has been your privilege to enjoy.
From what dangers he has rescued you—amidst
what temptations he has succored you—through
what difficulties he has conducted you—under
what trials he has supported you—and what
mercies he has showered upon you, during a
widowhood of thirty, forty, or fifty years! How
much of his power, wisdom, patience, faithfulness, and love, have you seen in all these varied
scenes, through which you have been called to
pass! Let it be the employment and delight
of your soul, in the long evening of your life,
to retrace, with gratitude and admiration, the
wondrous course and journey of your existence.
When by infirmity of body, you are shut out

from the public ordinances of religion, and the communion of the saints ; when through failing sight you can no longer read the Word of GOD, and you can only *think* upon its contents, dwell upon the past with thanksgiving and love. When you became a widow, perhaps early in life, you trembled, and asked, " How am I to be sustained ?" and lo ! there you are, a widow of threescore years and ten, or fourscore, acknowledging to the glory of GOD, that he has never left you, nor forsaken you.

And now, during the remainder of your days, and of your widowhood, withdraw your regards from this world, and prepare for that glory, on the verge of which you are now living. Almost every tie to earth is cut, or hangs very loose about your heart. Heaven has been accumulating its treasures, and multiplying its attractions for many years, and earth growing poorer and poorer, till one should suppose it has scarcely any thing now left to make you, as you retire from it, cast one lingering longing look behind. Let it be seen that you are dwelling on the border land, waiting and longing to pass

over.   Let it not distress you, if you cannot be
so vigorous in the service of GOD, as you once
were.   Do not be cast down, if you cannot hear
with the same attention—pray with the same
length, fixedness of thought, and fervour of
emotion; or that you cannot remember with
the same power and accuracy, as you once did.
It is the decay of nature, rather than the decline
of grace, and your divine Lord, will make the
same kind excuse for you, which he once did
for his slumbering disciples, and say, "The
spirit indeed is willing, but the flesh is weak."
Be it your aim, in a peculiar sense, to live by
faith.   You must have been long since weaned,
or ought to have been, from living upon frames
and feelings.   *Your* frames and feelings have
far less of liveliness than they once had, and
you must be brought to a simpler and firmer
reliance upon the faithfulness and unchange-
ableness of GOD.   You must rest upon the
simple promise, and rely upon the pure and
unmixed word.   Aged saint, believe, believe:
hold on to the end by faith.   By faith lay hold
of GOD's strength, to support your faltering
steps, and sustain you to the end.

Be as cheerful as you can, for the smiles of an aged christian, happy in the Lord, are as beautiful as the oblique rays of the setting sun, of a midsummer's day. Yes, though an aged widow, apparently forlorn and desolate, send forth notes of cheerful praise. Like good old ANNA, who when she came in and saw the Lord, gave thanks, and spake of CHRIST to those around; so do you. Encourage the younger widows to put their trust in GOD. Tell them how he has appeared for you. Bear testimony for him, and remind them he is the same yesterday, to-day, and for ever.

Let it appear to all who come round you, that though GOD sees fit to detain you upon earth, your affections have gone on before you into heaven; that your heart is dead, though your body lives; that though you are willing to wait all the days of your appointed time, till your change comes, that still the coming of the change will be a joyful moment. It is an unseemly sight, to behold an aged widow clinging to earth, even when its attractions, one should think, are gone; and loving the world, when its charms are all faded, and it is but the skeleton of what it was.

But, at the same time, let there be no impatience to be gone. Your husband is dead; perhaps your children also, and there be few in whom your heart takes a deep interest. *You* can see no reason why you should linger and loiter another hour in the world, which is one vast sepulchre, where all that was dear to you lies buried, and why, therefore, should such a tomb be your dwelling place ? Just because it is GOD's will to keep you here. Let there be no peevish wishes after death—no querulous complaints of life. It may be you are dependent, and are afraid you are a burden to your friends ; and this adds to your impatience to be gone— but strive against it. GOD loves his children too well to keep them one moment longer from his house and home above, than is best for his glory and their happiness.

# THIRD PART.

## LETTERS TO AND FROM WIDOWS.

# LETTERS TO WIDOWS.

THE first which I shall introduce is an extract of a letter from the Rev. JOHN HOWE, to Lady RACHEL RUSSELL, shortly after the execution of her husband. The whole letter is too long for insertion, but is well worthy of perusal, being one of the noblest and most pathetic pieces of epistolary composition in our language.

" MADAM,

* * * "It is, then, upon the whole, most manifest, that no temporary affliction whatsoever, upon one who stands in special relation to GOD, as a reconciled (and which is consequent an adopted) person, though attended with the most aggravating circumstances, can justify such a sorrow, so deep or so continued, as shall prevail against, and shut out a religious holy joy, or hinder it from being the prevailing principle in such a one. What can make that sor-

row allowable or innocent, what event of providence, (that can, whatever it is, be no other than an accident to our christian state,) that shall resist the most natural design and end of christianity itself? that shall deprave and debase the truly christian temper, and disobey and violate most express christian precepts? subvert the constitution of CHRIST's kingdom among men, and turn this earth (the place of GOD's treaty with the inhabitants of it, in order to their reconciliation to himself, and to the reconciled, the portal and gate of heaven; yea, and where the state of the very worst and most miserable has some mixture of good in it, that makes the evil of it less than that of hell) into a mere hell to themselves, of sorrow without mixture, and wherein shall be nothing but weeping and wailing.

The cause of your sorrow, madam, is exceeding great. The causes of your joy are inexpressibly greater. You have infinitely more left than you have lost. Doth it need to be disputed whether GOD be better and greater than man? or more to be valued, loved, and delighted in? and whether an eternal relation be more considerable than a temporary one? Was it not your constant sense in your best outward state? 'Whom have I in heaven but thee, O God; and whom can I desire on earth in comparison of thee!' Herein the state of your ladyship's case is still the same, (if you cannot rather with greater clearness, and with less hesitation pronounce those latter words.) The principal causes of your joy are immutable, such as no supervening thing can alter. You have lost a most pleasant, delectable earthly relative. Doth the blessed God hereby cease to be the best and most excellent good? Is his nature changed? his everlasting covenant reversed and annulled? which 'is ordered in all things and sure,' and is to be all your salvation and all your desire, 'whether he make your house on earth to grow or not to grow.' That sorrow which exceeds the proportion of its cause, compared with the remaining true and real causes of rejoicing, is, in that excess, causeless; that is, that excess of it wants a cause such as can justify or afford defence unto it.

P

\*   \*   \*   \*   \*   \*   \*   \*   \*   \*   \*

"Such as he hath pardoned, accepted, and prepared for himself, are to serve and glorify him in an higher and more excellent capacity, than they ever could in this wretched world of ours, and wherein they have themselves the highest satisfaction. When the blessed God is pleased in having attained and accomplished the end and intendments of his own boundless love, too great to be satisfied with the conferring of only temporary favours in this imperfect state, and they are pleased in partaking the full effects of that love; who are we, that we should be displeased? or that we should oppose our satisfaction to that of the glorious God, and his glorified creature? Therefore, madam, whereas you cannot avoid to think much on this subject, and to have the removal of that incomparable person, for a great theme of your thoughts, I do only propose most humbly to your honor, that you would not confine them to the sadder and darker part of that theme. It hath also a bright side; and it equally belongs to it, to consider whither he is gone, and to whom, as whence and from whom. Let, I beseech you, your mind be more exercised in contemplating the glories of that state your blessed consort is translated unto, which will mingle pleasure and sweetness with the bitterness of your afflicting loss, by giving you a daily intellectual participation, through the exercise of faith and hope, in his enjoyments. He cannot descend to share with you in your sorrows; you may thus every day ascend and partake with him in his joys. He is a pleasant subject to consider. A prepared spirit made meet for an inheritance with them that are sanctified, and with the saints in light, now entered into a state so connatural, and wherein it finds every thing most agreeable to itself. How highly grateful is it to be united with the true centre, and come home to the Father of spirits! To consider how pleasant a welcome, how joyful an entertainment he hath met with above! How delighted an associate he is with the general assembly, the innumerable company of angels, and the spirits of just men made perfect! How joyful an homage he continually pays to the throne of the celestial King!

" Will your ladyship think that an hard saying of our departing Lord to his mournful disciples, ' If ye loved me, ye would rejoice, that I said I go to the Father; for my Father is greater than I ?' As if he had said, he sits enthroned in higher glory than you can frame any conception of, by beholding me in so mean a condition on earth. We are as remote, and as much short in our thoughts as to the conceiving the glory of the supreme King, as a peasant, who never saw any thing better than his own cottage, from conceiving the splendour of the most glorious prince's court. But if that faith, which is the substance of things hoped for, and the evidence of things not seen, be much accustomed to its proper work and business—the daily delightful visiting and viewing the glorious invisible regions; if it be often conversant in those vast and spacious tracts of pure and brightest light, and amongst the holy inhabitants that replenish them; if it frequently employs itself in contemplating their comely order, perfect harmony, sublime wisdom, unspotted purity, most fervent mutual love, delicious con-

versation with one another, and perpetual pleasant consent in their adoration and observance
of their eternal King! who is there to whom it
would not be a solace to think I have such and
such friends and relatives, some, perhaps, as
dear as my own life, perfectly well pleased, and
happy among them! How can your love,
madam—so generous a love towards so deserving an object!—how can it but more fervently
sparkle in joy, for his sake, than dissolve in
tears for your own?

" Nor should such thoughts excite over-hasty
impatient desires of following presently into
heaven, but to the endeavours of serving GOD
more cheerfully on earth for our appointed
time: which I earnestly desire your ladyship
would apply yourself to, as you would not dis-
please GOD, who is your only hope, nor be cruel
to yourself, nor dishonour the religion of christians, as if they had no other consolations than
this earth can give, and earthly power take
from them. Your ladyship (if any one) would
be loth to do any thing unworthy of your family
and parentage. Your highest alliance is to

that Father and family above, whose dignity
and honour are, I doubt not, of highest account
with you.

"I multiply words, being loth to lose my
design; and shall only add that consideration
which cannot but be valuable with you upon
his first proposal, who had all the advantages
imaginable to give it its full weight; I mean
that of those dear pledges left behind. My
own heart even bleeds to think of the case of
those sweet babes, should they be bereaved of
their other parent too. And even your continued visible dejection would be their unspeakable disadvantage. You will always naturally
create in them a reverence of you; and I cannot but apprehend how the constant mien,
aspect, and deportment of such a parent will
insensibly influence the temper of dutiful children; and, if that be sad and despondent, de-
press their spirits, blunt and take off the edge
and quickness upon which their future usefulness and comfort will much depend. Were it
possible their now glorious father should visit
and inspect you, would you not be troubled to

behold a frown in that bright serene face ?  You
are to please a more penetrating eye, which you
will best do by putting on a temper and deportment suitable to your weighty charge and
duty; and to the great purposes for which GOD
continues you in the world, by giving over unnecessary solitude and retirement, which, though
it pleases, doth really prejudice you, and is more
than you can bear.  Nor can any rules of de-
cency require more.  Nothing that is necessary and truly christian, ought to be reckoned
unbecoming.  DAVID's example is of too great
authority to be counted a pattern of indecency.
The GOD of heaven lift up the light of his countenance upon you, and thereby put gladness
into your heart; and give you to apprehend
him saying to you, ' Arise and walk in the light
of the Lord.' "

I shall next introduce two of the most extra-
ordinary letters to be found in the page of history, both of which evince such a triumph of
faith over the feelings of humanity, as to be
admirably adapted to instruct and comfort all
that mourn.

The Rev. CHRISTOPHER LOVE, was a Presbyterian minister during the Commonwealth, a member of the Westminster Assembly of Divines, and one of the London ministers who united in a protest against the death of CHARLES THE FIRST. He was afterwards engaged, with many others, in a scheme to forward the return of CHARLES THE SECOND to England. All correspondence with the exiled monarch, having been declared treason by Act of Parliament, Mr. LOVE, upon the detection of the plot, was tried, convicted, and condemned as a traitor. In his conduct, whatever might be thought of it by others, he was influenced by conscientious motives, for all accounts concur, in bearing testimony to his character as an eminent christian. Great intercessions were made to the Parliament for the preservation of his life. These all failed, and he was beheaded on Tower Hill.

On the day before his death, his wife addressed to him the following letter:—*

* LIVES OF THE PURITANS, by Rev. B. BROOK, vol. iii. p. 129—132.

" ' My heavenly dear,

"I call thee so, because GOD hath put heaven into thee before he hath taken thee to heaven. Thou now beholdest GOD, CHRIST, and glory, as in a glass ; but to-morrow heaven's gates will be opened, and thou shalt be in the full enjoyment of all those glories which eye hath not seen, nor ear heard, neither can the heart of man understand. GOD hath now swallowed up thy heart in the thoughts of heaven ; but ere long thou shalt be swallowed up in the enjoyment of heaven ! And no marvel there should be such quietness and calmness in thy spirit, whilst thou art sailing in this tempestuous sea, because thou perceivest by the eye of faith, a haven of rest, where thou shalt be richly laden with all the glories of heaven ! O, lift up thy heart with joy, when thou layest thy dear head on the block, in the thoughts of this, that thou art laying thy head to rest in thy Father's bosom ; which, when thou dost awake, shall be crowned, not with an earthly, fading crown, but with an heavenly, eternal crown of glory ! Be not troubled when thou

shalt see a guard of soldiers triumphing with
their trumpets about thee; but lift up thy
head, and thou shalt behold GOD with a guard
of holy angels triumphing to receive thee to
glory! Be not dismayed at the scoffs and re-
proaches thou mayest meet with in thy short
way to heaven; for, be assured, GOD will not
only glorify thy body and soul in heaven, but
he will also make the *memory of thee to be glorious on earth !*

"O, let not one troubled thought for thy
wife and babes rise within thee! thy GOD will
be our GOD and our portion. He will be a
husband to thy widow, and a father to thy children: the grace of thy GOD will be sufficient
for us.

"Now, my dear, I desire willingly and
cheerfully to resign my right in thee to thy
Father and my Father, who hath the greatest
interest in thee: and confident I am, though
men have separated us for a time, yet GOD will
ere long bring us together again, where we
shall eternally enjoy one another, never to part
more!

" O, let me hear how GOD bears up thy heart, and let me taste of those comforts which support thee, that they may be as pillars of marble to bear up my sinking spirit! I can write no more. Farewell, farewell, my dear, till we meet where we shall never bid farewell more; till which time I leave thee in the bosom of a loving, tender-hearted Father; and so I rest,

" Till I shall for ever rest in heaven,

" MARY LOVE."

" This excellent letter discovers the same triumph over the world in Mrs. LOVE, which her husband so happily experienced. She was not only surrounded by their three children, but with child of a fourth; yet she passed over this circumstance in silence; and though formerly weak in grace, yet she now enjoyed strong confidence and great comfort, and animated her husband by the most encouraging considerations. Thus, 'by faith, out of weakness, she was made strong.' The next morning, being the day on which he suffered, Mr.

LOVE returned her the following farewell epistle :—

" My most gracious beloved,

    " I am now going from a prison to a palace. I have finished my work; I am now to receive my wages. I am going to heaven, where there are two of my children; and leaving thee on earth, where there are three of my babes : those two above need not any care; but the three below need thine. It comforts me to think two of my children are in the bosom of ABRAHAM, and three of them will be in the arms and care of so tender and godly a mother ! I know thou art a woman of a sorrowful spirit, yet be comforted. Though thy sorrows be great for thy husband's going out of the world, yet thy pains shall be the less in bringing thy child into the world : thou shalt be a joyful mother, though thou art a sad widow ! GOD hath many mercies in store for thee : the prayers of a dying husband will not be lost. To my shame I speak it, I never prayed so much for thee at liberty, as I have done in prison. I cannot write more; but I have a few practical counsels to leave with thee, viz.—

" 1. Keep under a sound, orthodox, and soul-searching ministry. O there are many deceivers gone out into the world; but CHRIST's sheep know his voice, and a stranger will they not follow. Attend on that ministry which teaches the way of GOD in truth, and follow SOLOMON's advice: *cease to hear the instruction that causeth to err from the way of knowledge.*

" 2. Bring up thy children in the knowledge and admonition of the Lord. The mother ought to be the teacher in the father's absence. *The words which his mother taught him.* TIMOTHY was instructed by his grandmother LOIS, and his mother EUNICE.

" 3. Pray in thy family daily, that thy dwelling may be in the number of the families that do call upon GOD.

" 4. Labour for a meek and quiet spirit, which is in the sight of GOD of great price.

" 5. Pore not on the comforts thou wantest; but on the mercies thou hast.

" 6. Look rather to God's end in afflicting, than at the measure and degree of thy afflictions.

" 7. Labour to clear up thy evidences for heaven, when God takes from thee the comforts of earth; that, as thy sufferings do abound, so thy consolations in Christ may much more abound.

" 8. Though it is good to maintain a holy jealousy of the deceitfulness of thy heart, yet it is evil for thee to cherish fears and doubts about the truth of thy graces. If ever I had confidence touching the graces of another, I have confidence of grace in thee. I can say of thee, as Peter did of Sylvanus, *I am persuaded that this is the grace of God wherein thou standest.* Oh, my dear soul, wherefore dost thou doubt, whose heart hath been upright, whose walkings have been holy! I could venture my soul in thy soul's stead. Such confidence have I in thee!

" 9. When thou findest thy heart secure, presumptuous, and proud, then pore upon corruption more than upon grace: but when thou findest thy heart doubting and unbelieving, then look on thy graces, not on thy infirmities.

" 10. Study the covenant of grace and merits of CHRIST, and then be troubled if thou canst. Thou art interested in such a covenant that accepts the righteousness of another, viz. that of JESUS CHRIST, as if it were our own. Oh my love, rest, rest then in the love of GOD, in the bosom of CHRIST!

" 11. Swallow up thy will in the will of GOD. It is a bitter cup we are to drink, but it is the cup our Father hath put into our hands. When PAUL was to go to suffer at Jerusalem, the christians could say, *The will of the Lord be done.* O say thou, when I go to Tower-hill, *The will of the Lord be done.*

" 12. Rejoice in my joy. To mourn for me inordinately, argues that either thou enviest or suspectest my happiness. *The joy of the Lord is my strength.* O, let it be thine also! Dear wife, farewell! I will call thee *wife* no more: I shall see thy face no more; yet I am not much troubled; for now I am going to

meet the bridegroom, the LORD JESUS CHRIST,
to whom I shall be eternally married!

" Thy dying,

" Yet most affectionate friend till death,

" CHRISTOPHER LOVE."

" From the Tower of London,

     " August 22, 1651,

" The day of my glorification."

Widows, read this, and learn submission to
the will of GOD, and heroic fortitude under his
afflictive hand.

## LETTERS FROM WIDOWS.

From MRS. HUNTINGTON, widow of an American Minister; describing the scene of MR. HUNTINGTON's death, and her own behaviour at the time: a bright proof of the power of prayer.

"Mr. HUNTINGTON was apprised, by the physician, of my arrival. There was an increase of ten to the number of his pulse upon this intelligence. When I entered the room in which he lay, he was gasping for breath; but his countenance glowed with an expression of tenderness I shall never forget, as he threw open his arms, exclaiming, 'My dear wife!' and clasped me, for some moments, to his bosom. I said, with perfect composure, 'My blessed husband, I have come at last.' He replied, 'Yes; and it is infinite mercy to me.' I told him, all I regretted was that I could not get to

Q

him sooner. He said, with a tender consideration for my health, which he always valued
more than his own, 'I am glad you could not ;
in your present circumstances it might have
been too much for me.'

"From that time, owing to the insidious
nature of his disease, I had considerable hope.
I had seen him. I was with him. He was as
sensible of my love and of my attentions as ever;
and I could not realise the stroke that was im-
pending. Never shall I remember without
gratitude the goodness of GOD in giving me
that last week of sweet, though sorrowful intercourse with my beloved husband.

"The days and nights of solicitude drew near
a fatal close. I could not think of his death.
At that prospect nature revolted. I felt as if
it would be comparatively easy to die for him.
But the day before his death, when all spoke
encouragement, I felt that we must part. In
the bitterness of my soul I went into the garret.
It was the only place I could have without
interruption. Never shall I forget that hour.
Whether in the body or out, I could scarcely

tell. I DREW NEAR TO GOD. Such a view of
the reality and nearness of eternal things I had
never had. It seemed as if I was somewhere
with GOD. I cast my eye back on this life, it
seemed a speck. I felt that GOD was my GOD,
and my husband's GOD; that this was enough;
that it was a mere point of difference whether
he should go to heaven first or I, seeing we
should both go so soon. My mind was filled
with satisfaction with the government of GOD.
' Be ye followers of them who, through faith
and patience, inherit the promises,' seemed to
be the exhortation given me upon coming back
to this world. I do not mean that there were
any bodily or sensible appearances. But I
seemed carried away in the spirit. I pleaded
for myself and children travelling through this
distant country. It seemed as if I gave them,
myself, and husband up entirely; and it was
made sure to me that GOD would do what was
best for us.

From that time, though nature would have
her struggles, I felt that GOD had an infinite
right to do what he pleased with his own; that

Q 2

he loved my husband better than I did; that if he saw him ripe for his rest, I had no objections to make. All the night he was exercised with expiring sufferings, and GOD was pouring into my soul one truth and promise of the gospel after another. I felt it sweet for him to govern. There was a solemn tranquillity filled the chamber of death. It was an hour of extremity to one whom JESUS loved. I felt that He was there, that angels were there, that every agony was sweetened and mitigated by ONE, in whose sight the death of his saints is precious. I felt as if I had gone with the departing spirit to the very utmost boundary of this land of mortals, and as if it would be easier for me to drop the body which confined my soul in its approach towards heaven, than retrace all the way I had gone. When the intelligence was brought to me that the conflict was over, it was good news—I kissed the clay, as pleasantly as I ever did when it was animated by the now departed spirit. I was glad he had got safely home, and that all the steps of his departure were so gently ordered.

"It would be in vain for me to attempt a description of my feelings the next morning. I had never seen such a sun rise before. It beheld me alone. Were I the only created being in the universe, I could not, perhaps, have felt very differently. I went into the chamber in which he died. There, on the pillow was the print of his head. The bed of death was just as when it resigned for ever the body of him who was all the world to me. His portmanteau, comb, brush, et cet. lay in sight. GOD wonderfully supported me.

"But why do I dwell on a description which even now is almost too much for me? How did GOD sustain a creature who was weakness itself! How mercifully he has carried me through all my successive trials! Truly it was the Lord's doing: and it is marvellous in my eyes.

"And now, oh how is it now? Not so much comfort; labouring with sin; afraid almost to live in this wicked world; dreading a thousand evils in my present lonely state. But all this is wrong. GOD hath said, 'Who shall harm you, if ye be followers of that which is good ?' How kindly my beloved husband used to remind me of this text !"

## TO A FRIEND WHO HAD LOST A NEAR RELATION.

"Your long and confidential letter gave me great pleasure. There is a sympathy in the feeling of persons who have been recently afflicted, which cannot be expected to be found in others; a mutual chord, which, touched, vibrates with a kindred sound. We have not suffered exactly alike; but we have suffered; and that circumstance has made us love each other better than we did before. *   *   *   *   *

"When I view myself, riven asunder, root and branch, not the limbs torn away, but the very body of the tree sundered from top to bottom, nature must feel the parting agonies, must at times, be ready to sink under the consciousness of her dissolution. All this must be to those who have interests to be smitten, friendships to be broken. and hearts to feel.

Yes, dear E——, our hearts have bled. The wound inflicted has been deep. We have felt

that the stroke was full of anguish, that it went
to our very souls. We will not deny that this
is all true. We will not please ourselves with
the delusion that the deep, deep wound which
the hand of GOD has inflicted, can ever cease to
bleed. But, O my friend! 'is there not balm
in Gilead? is there not a physician there?' Is
not that physician our Saviour; wise to discern,
prudent to manage, strong to save? Has not
the kind hand which smote so deeply, accompanied the stroke with many softening, mitigat-
ing circumstances? Oh yes; I trust we both feel
that it is so. It is GOD who hath afflicted us,
the infinitely wise, compassionate, and faithful
Jehovah, the Lord our GOD. And does it not
argue great want of confidence in him, if we sink
into despondency when he chastises us? Does
it not show, either that we think we could
manage things better than he can, or that there
is something which we have not cordially submitted to his disposal?

"And now, O GOD, thou art the potter, and
we the clay. O how this quells the murmurings
of self-will; how it settles the restlessness of

the troubled spirit; how it plucks the sting from
the rod of affliction! GOD knows best. Precious truth! It is an anchor to the soul, sure
and steadfast, which keeps it from shipwreck,
amidst all the storms and tempests of the
troubled sea of life. Oh, for a firm, unwavering faith! This is all that is wanting. With
this we may say,

Cheerful I tread the desert through.

With this we may rejoice when our beloved
friends are taken from the stormy ocean to the
peaceful port, from the weary wilderness to the
happy home, from the field of conflict to the
crown of victory; and trace with holy courage,
our way through the same difficulties to the
same glorious recompence of reward. But, ah!
this, a firm unwavering faith, is too often wanting. We miss our temporal comforts. The
heart which sympathised in all our pleasures
and pains, has ceased to beat; the ear which
was always open to listen to our complaints and
wishes, is closed; the kind voice of affection
and disinterested love, is hushed; the arm

which supported us, is withdrawn.   It is a chilling thought.   Cherished alone, we feel its freezing, benumbing influence fastening upon all the springs of comfort and hope, and turning every stream of joy into one waste of cold and motionless despair.

"But, my dear friend, we must not view our trials thus.   We must think much and often of the blessedness of those whose removal we lament, of the perfection of the divine government, of the certainty of the promise, that ' all things shall work together for good to them that love God,' of the rapid approach of that hour which will unite us eternally to those in Christ whom we love, of the danger of creature-comforts, and of the suffering life on earth of our glorious High-priest and head, and his assurance that it is through much tribulation we must enter the kingdom.   Oh, my dear E——, if we are christians, there is a glorious prospect before us—as much of the good things of this life as an infinitely wise and kind Father sees to be best for us, and hereafter an eternity of unmingled and ineffable bliss !"

TO A SISTER-IN-LAW.

*" Boston, Sept.* 22, 1819.

" I received your kind letter, my dear sister, this forenoon. I am happy to say I have passed the time, since you left me, much more comfortably than I expected. GOD is very gracious to me. He gives me such a measure of sweet quietness, as composes and tranquillises my spirits. ' Blessed is the man who trusteth in the Lord, and whose hope the Lord is : for he shall be as a tree planted by the waters, and that spreadeth out her roots by the river, and shall not see when heat cometh, but her leaf shall be green ; and shall not be careful in the year of drought, neither shall cease from yielding fruit.' Sometimes I have fears that the precious promises of GOD's Word cannot belong to one so vile and rebellious. But I am generally able to flee to the blood of sprinkling—to trust in Him in whom all the promises of GOD are yea and amen, and to say, ' Lord, thou knowest all things ; thou knowest that I love thee.' Yes, my dear sister, on GOD's part all is mercy, mercy ! The world has changed with me. But the memory of the blessed saint is pleasant, though mournful to the soul. The prospect of heaven makes the dark shades of my picture brighter. * * * * * * *

"*September* 25. The desolating stroke my soul was dreading, when I last wrote in this journal, has fallen upon me. Yes, it has fallen upon me—and I live! What shall I say? The right hand of the Lord doeth valiantly, or I should now have dwelt in silence. Wonderful grace! He that hath loved me bore me through. His everlasting arm was under me. He taught and enabled me to say, 'Thy will be done.' To him be glory. The being I loved better than myself has left me in this wilderness. He on whom I leaned has gone over the Jordan. But another arm, mightier than his, sustains me. I can say, I humbly believe, with truth, 'Nevertheless I am not alone, for GOD is with me.' And I must again cry, Grace! grace! I am a wonder to myself. Oh the infinite grace of GOD! A worm is in the furnace and is not consumed! And must I not love this 'strong Deliverer'

better than all ?    Shall I not cheerfully give up
my comforts at his command ?

" *October* 3.    When I can, I intend writing
some of the particulars of my blessed husband's
departure, for future satisfaction, should I live.
When I look at my loss only, I sink.    What I
lost in that holy man of GOD, that amiable companion, that faithful friend, that prudent counsellor, that devoted husband, GOD knows!
What the church has lost, in his eminent con-
secration of himself to his work, his love to the
poor, his compassion to the afflicted, his meekness and humility, his zeal and disinterestedness, his fervent prayers, his lovely and almost
spotless example, GOD knows!    Oh it is pleasant for memory to dwell on the recollection of
what he was !    'Tis a beautiful picture, on which
I must ever fasten the eye of my fond remembrance with satisfaction.    But that light is removed: put out, I do not say.    Oh no!    He
lives to die no more.    And I am permitted to
hope I shall, ere long, go to him, and dwell
with him for ever in heaven !    GOD is carrying
on an infinitely perfect plan of government.

The removal of my beloved husband, in the midst of his usefulness, is a part of that plan. Shall I not lay my hand on my mouth, and say, ' Thy will be done ?' "

TO A FRIEND WHO HAD LOST HER HUSBAND.

*" Boston, January 25th.* 1820.

" My dear Friend and Sister,

        " Ever since that sorrowful event which numbered me among those who can more emphatically than other classes of mourners, say, " Lover and friend hast thou put far from me, and mine acquaintance into darkness," I have felt desirous of writing to you.    Not because I expected to offer any consolation to your mind, with which it is not already much better acquainted than mine, but from that natural feeling of sympathy, which is excited towards those whose trials are similar to our own.    And now that I have taken up my pen, the reflection that my time might be better occupied than in obtruding myself upon you, and thus opening anew the fountains of your grief ( if, indeed, they have ever been closed in any measure,) by

the recital of my own sufferings, almost induces
me to lay it down again.   However, I do not
mean to pain you, and agonize myself, in this
way.    Profitable  as  it  may  be  for  common
mourners, to dwell often and long upon the circumstances of their bereavements, in order to
cherish  the  impressions  which  such  dispensations may have made on their hearts, it is not
profitable for *us*.   Such sorrow as ours is in no
danger of being suddenly diverted.    The danger
is on the other side, of its pressing so constantly
and heavily on the spirit, as to crush the feeble
body to the grave.   And would it not have been
so with us, my dear friend, were it not that the
hand of the Lord has been upon us for good ?

   " I have wished, and still wish, to know how
you do, what are your circumstances, and how
your  mind  has  been  exercised  under  its  heavy
afflictions.    I, you know, have had accumulated
ones.    But have we not both found that precious
promise  verified,  'As  thy  days,  so  shall  thy
strength  be ?'    Has  the  Lord  ever  been  a
' wilderness' to us ?   And  may  we  not  safely
trust  him  for  the  future ?   Does he not know

exactly, what measure of sorrow we can bear, as well as what kind we need?

And now, my friend, what remains for us to do in this world? Not to live for the temporal enjoyments of life, certainly; for how can any comfort be received, any delight enjoyed, which will not, as long as we live, be embittered by the recollection of those, dearer to us than our own lives, who once sympathized in all our joys, and whose sympathy with us was a principal source of our satisfaction? Yes, this bitter, bitter thought will press itself upon our remembrance, when we lie down, and when we rise up, in the house, and by the way. And, viewing our loss only in this manner, the world looks like a waste, a desert, a weary monotonous desert, stripped of all that once enlivened it. But we must not view it so. What did CHRIST live for? What did PAUL live for? Alas! if we could find our happiness here in that in which the Saviour found his, we might yet see many good days in the land of the living. And this is what we must labour after. If we have little left us to enjoy, have we nothing left us to do? And the happiness of our souls ought to result, the happiness of a holy soul will result, from doing and being just what GOD pleases. The mind which feels that it has no sympathies to be exercised, no object upon which to repose its affections, no business to employ its faculties, must sink into a state of hopeless and dreadful despondency. But the Christian should never feel thus. Though our precious husbands have left us, have we nothing to feel or do for their children; nothing to do for CHRIST, and for the church which he hath purchased with his own blood? And may we not yet be happy in doing diligently the work which he has given us to do? My dear friend, we shall never be happy *just as* we have been. Oh, no, never. The smile of tenderness will wait for us no more when returning to our sorrowful habitations. The voice of unmingled love will greet us no more in our afflictions. The counsellors, advisers, supporters, and prophets, upon whom we leaned, who sanctioned by their influence the expressions of maternal authority, who bore us constantly and earnestly before GOD, are gone!

Nature shudders, as she casts her eye forward, and thinks of this long, long, long separation.

"But why have I suffered myself to fall into this sorrowful strain? I did it unintentionally, unconsciously. Forgive me. I have pained you, and I have pained myself. I was going to say, we must find our happiness in a different way—in girding up the loins of our mind to a more diligent performance of duty; in putting on, as good soldiers of the cross, the whole armour of GOD; in setting our faces as a flint against every thing which can discourage, intimidate, or wound us; in remembering the example of our devoted, our suffering Saviour, in leaning on his arm, confiding in his wisdom, and trusting in his grace and strength, and in sending forward our hearts to that happy, happy home, which we hope one day to reach, and whither our beloved friends have gone before us. Let our expectations of earthly rest be moderate, except of that sweet rest which results from simple trust in GOD.

"I have written thus far, and have not yet mentioned what I had most in view when I

R

began. I think we may derive benefit from remembering each other's children in our prayers. Can we not devote ten minutes every Saturday evening, at nine o'clock, to special prayer for each other, that we may have grace, wisdom, courage and patience to do our duty; and for our children, that their affections may be sanctified, our instructions blessed, they brought into the covenant early, et. cet? Will you write, and let me know what you think of it? My little boy wakes, and I must bid you adieu."

FROM LADY POWERSCOURT, WHO LOST HER HUSBAND ABOUT A YEAR AFTER THEIR MARRIAGE.*

### LETTER V.

"DEAR Mr. . . . . I should have answered your kind letter before this, had I any thing to tell you that could have given you any gratification. But alas! I have been as desolate

* The letters and papers of this eminent christian, and strong minded woman, as published by the Rev. ROBERT DALY, are a precious volume, full of instruction, consolation and reproof.

within, as without.  My earthly husband hid
from me, my heavenly one I cannot find; and
Satan hard at work tempting me to say, what
is this black thing I have done, which makes
my Father so angry with me?  But oh, my
dear Lord, let him not rule within : quench his
fiery darts : show me that I deserve far worse,
even all the wrath of an offended GOD.  But
JESUS has 'borne our griefs and carried our
sorrows.'  These trials are only blessings, to
fill up that which is behind of his afflictions.
I am also tempted to think, that I cannot be
his, for I feel none of that comfort his children
always feel, and I used to find in the hour of
trial. . . . . . JONAH, doest thou well to be
angry?  I will bear the indignation of the
Lord, because I have sinned grievously against
him.  Oh, dear Mr. . . . . . , you do not know
what it is to lose one so dear, so very dear; I
can only compare it to the tearing asunder all
the strings of the heart.  Then such a gloomy
prospect here the rest of one's life.  After
watching him day and night with so much
anxiety, anticipating the joy of being allowed

again to be with him; all at once so unexpect-
edly to have my hopes dashed from me, was
what I did not think for some days I could
have borne, because I forgot that as my day so
should my strength be.  In any other loss I
have had, I never could pray for the bodily life
of my friend, but in this, to which no other
loss can be compared, night and day I could
not help entreating the Lord to spare me that
heavy blow.  I really did think he meant to
answer me, and hoped against hope, till the last
breath left that dear body. . . . . But I know,
O Lord, that thy judgments are right, and that
in very faithfulness thou hast afflicted me—I
must wait to know and see why it is, till I
know as I am known.  That it is unspeakable
love, I have no doubt, because he who hath
sent it is no new friend, but a tried and precious one; and when it is good for me he will
allow me to see, that this GOD *is* Love.  But
oh, I tremble when I look at my rebellion, and
ingratitude, throughout it all.  I have had
much to show me myself this last year—to dig
up the mud hid under the smooth surface.

How will it astonish you—astonish angels, when the book of my sins is opened, except they are so blotted out with blood as to make them illegible.

"I do not suppose, there could be a stronger lesson of the vanity of every thing earthly, than to look at me, last year and this. The prospects of happiness I seemed to set out with! And now, where are they? A living monument that man in his best estate is altogether vanity —and see how my heart, without my knowing it was on earth. I could not have thought, one who professes to believe in the joys of heaven, and had tasted the realisation of them by faith, could so mourn, as one without hope— could so willingly call him back again. But I shall say no more, for these complaints only grieve my GOD, and annoy you. But, indeed, I am at times greatly oppressed, and feel this evening as if there were a parcel of devils within, tearing me different ways, and refusing me any rest. I beseech you pray for me, and write to me,

"Your unalterably affectionate

"And grateful friend,

"T. A. POWERSCOURT."

LETTER VI.

\*     \*     \*     \*     \*     \*

\*   \*   \*   " How I shall long to join you all
above.   I fear I need patience, and find it hard
to reconcile my mind to the possibility of my
living three times as long as I have lived yet.
When I look back upon a few months, and remember the happiness I used to feel when I
expected my dearest love, and  .  .  .  , to
spend the evening at .  .  .  . and to have a
little reading, I can hardly persuade myself that
I am the same person.   Two now in possession
of what they then, blessed be GOD, enjoyed by
faith, and I left alone.—But I forgot—I determined never to murmur again.   It needs a great
stretch of faith sometimes, when the enemy
comes in like a flood, to believe that GOD is as
much at peace with me through CHRIST, as
with those already above; that ABRAHAM now
in glory is not safer than I am.   Is that pre-
sumption do you think?   What a precious name,
a strong tower, into which, if we run, we shall
be safe !   Were I left to myself I should run
*from* it.   I would not trust myself to His word,

but seek to save myself from danger. But almighty love arrests me, pulls me in; and then rewards me for coming. How much in those words, '*are safe*,'—to think we are safe from every thing! No evil shall ever touch us, evil at the end, or evil on the way. All paved with love; 'all things shall work together for good.' I have got the promise of all others I want— '*let thy widows trust in me.*' I once wished there was a richer, a sweeter promise to widows; but I believe it requires to be brought into different circumstances, in order to feel the force of different promises. For the Lord knew that none so suited widows, as these few words. In looking round the wide world, so filled with wickedness, and seeing one has to pass through it alone, one would fear, every step one took so unprotected and forlorn, only for this promise. With this 'when I am weak, then am I strong.' It is not like Him to invite us to trust in him, and then let any evil come nigh us. If His everlasting arms are underneath, I 'shall dwell in safety alone.' Let there be rebellions, revolutions, persecutions, earthquakes, any thing,

every thing, '*let thy widows trust in me,*' should
be enough. I know my tabernacle shall be in
peace. Sweet to think that the eye of the Lord
is upon us, to deliver our souls from death. It
seems to me, as a nurse keeps her eye upon
her child lest it should destroy itself, or as a
keeper keeps his eye upon his poor lunatic, 'the
Lord is thy keeper.' Then unbelief jumps up
and says, how do you know all this is for you?
Then I do not know what to say, but 'my Master told me so.' His Spirit witnesses with my
spirit. He has given me the earnest of the
Spirit. To those who believe, he is precious,
and I think he is precious to me—' a bundle of
myrrh is my well-beloved unto me.' Oh that
I could keep close to him; I want to be fixed
on the rock. My grief is, that the waves of sin
and the world, give me so many shoves off it.
Will you not pray for me, for I greatly need it;
and will you not write to me, and exhort me
with purpose of heart to cleave unto the Lord;
and tell me if you think me presumptuous, or
going wrong in any way. That old serpent is
so cunning. Will you forgive me for speaking

so much of myself, but speaking of what He can do for me, magnifies the power of his grace, more than if I was to speak of it with regard to any one else upon earth.

"Yours, with christian affection,

"T. A. POWERSCOURT."

LETTER VIII.

\*     \*     \*     \*     \*     \*

\*     \*     "I have to thank you for your other kind long letter. There is a certain drawing out of heart towards those who care enough for us, as to point out in what way we may be grieving our Lord. Your accusations, I fear, are quite just; and I hope I may have your prayers, that I may be enabled to walk worthy of the Lord unto all pleasing. I think it is in the Lord we are told to rejoice, a joy which can be felt while sorrowing, a good cheer in tribulation. I sometimes sit in astonishment, why my cup should run over with this blessing, and I have more when the heart is brought low to receive it, than when it is (which is often the case) intoxicated. I own I feel sometimes cast

down and desolate, but not unhappy. I have
had a deep, a very deep wound; the trial has
been very severe; but how should I have known
Him as a brother born for adversity, without
it? How should I prize him as my strength
if I am not sometimes left to feel my perfect
weakness? The heart is too selfish not to drop
a tear sometimes, but I hope no longer a rebellious one. The wound is closed, but very little
bursts it open. The marble must be allowed
to melt a little, but only enough to send to that
good physician, who maketh sore, and bindeth
up; he woundeth, and his hands make whole.
I understand these lines,

> " Cry and groan beneath afflictions,
>   Yet to dread the thoughts of ease."

However, if it is more to his glory, that I should
take pleasure in the many blessings left in this
world, dreary as it may seem through the glass
of affliction, 'behold I am here, Lord;'—if to
be kept low, even so. May I only be able to
lay this soul as helpless on the great 'I AM.'
And I can assure you, however appearances

may contradict it, I have much joy and peace in
believing, and find life a flux and reflux of love;
JESUS is precious to me. I find his banner of
love extended over Edinburgh : his promises
here also are as honey dropping from the comb.
There is not one on earth I desire but him; he
is all my hope and all my salvation; and I can
go on with confidence, knowing he can never
deny himself, or say, 'I never knew you,' for
he testifies not only that he knows me, but that
he loves me, by enabling me to say, 'thou
knowest all things, thou knowest that I love
thee.'

"Sometimes we appear such insignificant
grass-hoppers, that it is hard to conceive that
he can think of us and our foolish concerns; at
other times one feels of such immense importance, that one wonders that christians can live
like other people, such as when we read of the
bursts of joy from the heavenly host, and find
this the sign that their Lord whom they adore
has become a despised babe, and all, because
peace is brought to earth, and good will to man.
Peace seems just what we want here, purchased

by his blood, left as his legacy. What simplicity there seemed to be in his words after his resurrection. He seemed to enjoy the travail of his soul, when distributing his peace. May he impart largely of it to your soul, and while recommending the inexpressible treasure of his word to others, may you be enabled yourself to feed on it, by faith with thanksgiving. May he empty of his fulness into all our bosoms, and enable us by using, to show we value the privilege of drawing near to him, to tell him of fear the world cannot allay, of wants the world cannot satisfy, of blessings the world knows nothing of.

"Your affectionate,

"T. A. Powerscourt."

## LETTER IX.

\* \* \* "Is your happy soul still lifted up? able in his light to walk through darkness? I know the dreary waste that lies before you. How his dear, dear company is missed—how tasteless and insipid every thing appears—how you want that affection which entered into every

trifle which concerned you—how you want an
adviser, a protector, such a companion—one to
weep when you weep—to rejoice when you rejoice.   I know well what it is to lie down at
night and say, where is he?—to awake in the
morning, and find him gone—to hear the hour
strike day after day, at which you once expected
his daily return home to his too happy fire-side
—and find nothing but a remembrance that
embitters all the future here.   Oh my poor,
poor . . . . if I cannot feel for you, who can?
—who so often partook of your happiness?—
sweet, precious time I have been allowed to
enjoy with you both, but *past*.   However, it is
well that you have another to feel for you.   If
I know the meaning of the word sorrow, I also
know of a joy a stranger intermeddleth not with.
How tenderly our compassionate Lord speaks
of the widow! as a parent who feels the punishment more than the chastened child.   He
seems intent to fill up every gap love has been
forced to make: one of his errands from heaven was to bind up the broken-hearted.   He
has an answer for every complaint you may

ever be tempted to make. Do you say you have none now to follow, to walk with, to lean on ? He will follow you and invite you to come up from the wilderness leaning on him as your beloved. Is it that you want one to be interested in all your concerns ? Cast all your cares upon him, for he careth for you. A protector ? Let thy widows trust in me. An adviser ? Wonderful Counsellor ! Companion ? I will not leave you comfortless ; I will come unto you ; I will never leave you, nor forsake you ; I have not called you servants but friends ; behold I stand at the door and knock, if any man hear my voice, and open the door, I will come in unto him, and sup with him, and he with me. One to weep with you ? In all their affliction he was afflicted ; JESUS wept. When you lie down —safe under the shadow of his wings, under the banner of his love. When you awake— still about your path and about your bed. It is worth being afflicted to become intimately acquainted, and to learn to make use of, the chief of ten thousand—the altogether lovely—the brother born for adversity—the friend that sticketh closer than a brother—the friend of sinners. Pray write often to your poor sister; tell me of every thing that interests you; do do not let the children forget me." . . . .

From Mrs. LEWIS, widow of the Rev. MICHAEL LEWIS, Missionary to the Negroes, Demarara, to her widowed mother.

" My dear and honoured mother,

" Surely I am bereaved! O yes, I am bereaved! But of what—of whom am I bereaved? Of a dear, a tender, an affectionate husband; of a mother, a friend, a brother. All these relations in him I found combined, but he is gone! My soul be still and know that all is well; rejoice that he who first gave thee such a treasure, has seen fit to recall him. O, I would not for one moment repine. It is true, I had fondly hoped to have had him spared to me for a few more years. Two short years and eleven days had just expired since we together left our dear widowed mother for a far distant land, when my dear husband was welcomed to the skies. My dearest Saviour, thou didst call him, and he is gone to receive that crown which fadeth not, the assurance of which cheers my very heart, because he will weep no more. Sorrow and sighing are for ever flown from him. I know too that my Redeemer liveth, and that soon the same voice that sweetly called the darling of my heart from this vale of tears, to mansions in the upper and better world, will say to her that is left to mourn her loss, 'Weep no more, but come up hither and enter into the joy of your Lord.' *Pray, pray,* for your REBECCA.

"I would fain attempt to describe the death-bed scene of my dearest earthly love; but I find it impossible to do so. The joy, the bliss indeed was great. This line was constantly in my mind, 'O the pain, the bliss of dying.' Yes; it deserved the name of bliss, for it was bliss supremely great. Not one cloud was permitted to veil his sky; enough to silence every rising painful thought; and through mercy I can assure you, my dearest mother, it has. The Lord made good his promise to me when my heart was nearly overwhelmed in prospect of a separation taking place between us; he was pleased to make my dearest husband the medium through which to afford consolation, and to impart submission. Yes, two days before his happy spirit took its flight, on seeing me rather cast down and very anxious, accompanied with the trickling tear which stole down my face, he said to me, with looks indicating marked affection, and with a soft tone of voice, ready to join his voice with mine,—' O naughty, naughty,—you know, my dear, if this is the time the Lord is about to separate us from each other, we should try to feel quite submissive to his righteous will, for he does all things well.' I felt reproved and retired to bless the Lord for his great kindness in giving my dearest husband such sweet submission to his holy will; and to entreat that the same blessing might be bestowed upon myself; nor did the hearer and answer of prayer turn a deaf ear to the voice of my supplication, for while I was yet speaking he answered me; and after this, it mattered not who tried to persuade me that the Lord would still spare him to me, for I had quite

s

given him up to his entire, and gracious disposal.    *    *    *    *    *

"As I was withdrawing from his bed-side, he said in a low tone of voice, not intending I should hear him, 'Ah, I am sorry for thee, my dear.' I was determined he should not see me weeping, lest he should think I was sorrowing, and spoke to him as firmly as possible. About seven o'clock he said, 'My love, I hope your tears are tears of gratitude.' I answered 'yes, they are tears of gratitude.' 'O that is quite right, quite right,' and seemed to say 'Weep on then.'—This was no small mercy to me, as weeping seemed to relieve me of such a burden.

    *    *    *    *    *    *

" 'I shall be with you in spirit,' he said, 'though absent in body.' 'Yes, my dear,' I replied, 'you are about to leave us and go to that blessed JESUS to receive the early crown you have been speaking to us about so often lately.'    *    *    *    *    *

" I observed 'you seem longing to clap your glad wings and fly away to seats prepared above.' 'I am, I am! my dear; tell them to sing—

'Praise ye the Lord, our hearts shall join,
 In work so pleasant so divine,
Now while the flesh is my abode,
 And when my soul ascends to GOD.'

When we came to the sixth verse—

'He helps the stranger in distress,
The widow and the fatherless ;'

It was almost too much for all, but his dear self.   *   *   *   *   *

"He remained silent for a little time—then my ears caught the sound 'Come Lord JESUS, come.' The people gradually returned into the room again, he said 'Sing, Salvation, O the joyful sound;' we sang it—he then sweetly addressed us from the word salvation, and said it would probably be the last time he should do so. The address was pathetic indeed, it was about half an hour long. To sergeant ADAMS he said, 'Pray, pray,' he knelt and prayed in a very affecting manner. My dearest LEWIS kept adding his amen to the petition. As we arose from our knees he exclaimed, 'Sing, sing, —'Salvation, O the joyful sound,' again, with

s 2

the chorus.' At the end of each verse we sang the chorus, it was as follows,—

> ' Glory, honour, praise and power,
>     Be unto the Lamb for ever !
> JESUS CHRIST is our Redeemer,
>     Hallelujah ! Praise the Lord.'

"As we were singing the chorus the last time, he began to sing the word Hallelujah, on earth,—but went to heaven to finish it ! but I finished it and added, ' Praise ye the Lord.' I felt my life ought to be a life of praise. Thus the dear departed breathed his last, without a long-fetched breath—his end was peace. With mine own hand I closed his eyes on the twenty-second of January, exactly at twelve o'clock in the day, (the Sabbath.) Dear man of GOD, much as I loved and still love thee, I rejoice that thou hast entered into thy rest.

"My dear mother, weep not because REBECCA is left a widow in a strange land ; rather rejoice that my heart has something like a loadstone drawing it towards heaven ; for there my best friends and kindred dwell, there GOD my Saviour reigns."

And now, in conclusion, what can I add for your instruction or comfort, except it be a few words on that blessed, though mysterious union, which exists between CHRIST and his believing people. Looking sorrowfully, as you now do, on the broken bonds of that close and tender union, which was once the source of your chief earthly happiness, and the dissolution of which has left you a lonely pilgrim, in this world's great wilderness, comfort yourself with the thought, that if joined unto the Lord by faith, and made one spirit with *him,* there is at least one union which even *death* cannot dissolve, and one tie which nothing can weaken or rupture. How tender and how beautiful is the representation, which sets forth CHRIST as the husband of his church. You can feel this now, as you never felt it before. He not only loves you with an affection, to which even that of your husband was cold, but will *ever live* to manifest his affection. Death has severed you from your earthly husband, but it can never take from you this heavenly bridegroom. Standing at the grave of all that was most dear to you on

earth, and reading in mournful silence, and
with many tears, that simple record of mortality upon his tomb, which contains the history and the date of your sorrows, take up the
triumphant exultation of the apostle, and exclaim, "Nay, in all these things we are more
than conquerors, through him that hath loved us;
for I am persuaded that neither death, nor life,
nor angels, nor principalities, nor powers, nor
things present, nor things to come, nor height,
nor depth, nor any other creature, shall be able
to separate us from the love of GOD, which is
in CHRIST JESUS our Lord.—Rom. viii. 37—
39.   Nor is this the language of vain boasting,
but of well founded confidence.   No, nothing
shall burst the bond, which unites the redeemed
soul to its redeeming Saviour.   This Divine
Head will hold in close, vital, and inseparable
union, every member that is incorporated into
him by faith.   And as *you* cannot be severed by death from CHRIST, so neither is your
departed husband, if he were a true believer.
The righteous sleep in JESUS.   In death they
are still one with him.   The spirit has been

disunited from its mortal and corruptible body, but not from its immortal and incorruptible head. All the rights and privileges which belong to believers, in virtue of their union with CHRIST, remain with them in and after death undiminished, unimpaired. Dead they are, but they are dead in CHRIST: they are as much comprehended in his covenant; summed up in him as their head; represented by him as their advocate, as they possibly could be, while here on earth. Whatever is meant by their being in CHRIST, is meant of them now they are dead, and shall be made good to them at his appearing. Wherefore you are one with him you have lost still: you meet in CHRIST's spiritual body, and are bound by a mystical tie in the same sacred fellowship.

What is to follow? The heavenly bridegroom will take home his bride to his mansions of glory, which he is gone to prepare for the object of his love. How tender, yet how sacred and how solemn is the adjuration of the apostle, where he says, " Now we beseech you, brethren, by the coming of our Lord JESUS CHRIST, and

by *our gathering together unto him."*—2 Thess.
ii. 1.    There is now a scattering, but then
there is to be a gathering.   His chosen, redeemed, regenerated, sanctified church, now
severed from each other, though still united in
him, shall be then collected into his presence,
and gathered round his throne; not one of its
members shall be missing, but the spiritual body
will be complete with its Divine Head.    Mortality will be swallowed up of life.    Heaven will
be a region of vitality; a living world, a world
of life.    The widow's GOD shall be there, but
not the widow, *as* a widow.    Her tears will be
wiped away; her loss will be repaired; her
sorrows will be turned into joy, for she will be
associated again with the companion of her pilgrimage; not indeed in the bonds of a fleshly
union, but in the ties of a spiritual fellowship;
for they shall be as the angels of GOD, and shall
dwell together for ever in that glorious state, of
which it is said, *there,* SHALL BE NO MORE
DEATH.

B. HUDSON, PRINTER, BULL STREET, BIRMINGHAM.